T0328069

A House With A Date Palm Will Never Starve

لا يجوع اهله بيت فيه نخيل

Michael Rakowitz and Friends

A HOUSE WITH A DATE PALM WILL NEVER STARVE

Cooking With Date Syrup

Forty-One Chefs and an Artist Create New and Classic
Dishes with a Traditional Middle Eastern Ingredient

ART/BOOKS **Plinth**

Contents

Foreword

I first met Michael in 2017 at a dinner he organized in the beautiful garden of the A. M. Qattan Foundation in South Kensington. It was a magical occasion, completely enthralling. Michael, aided by his friends Ella and Regine, cooked for a large number of people a traditional Iraqi-Jewish meal in huge saucepans in the open air. He gave me an apron embroidered with my name and said that I had inspired his cooking, which made me very happy. I sat at a table with a Saudi woman, a Syrian woman, and an Iraqi-Jewish architect. The food kept coming. For starters, we had pickled mango salad, dried broad beans with lemon, *sambusak* (little pies) filled with fried onions and chickpeas, and dates stuffed with walnuts. The mains were from Michael's grandmother's recipes. *Ingriyyi*, a dish of minced lamb cooked with onion, tomato, and aubergine, had a delicate taste of tamarind. *Kubba shwandar*, a sweet-and-sour beetroot stew with meat-filled dumplings, was accompanied by turmeric and saffron rice with raisins and almonds.

Michael organizes these meals regularly. His project called *Dar Al Sulh*, or 'Domain of Conciliation', began in 2013 as a pop-up restaurant in Dubai. It was the first in the Arab world to serve the cuisine of Iraqi Jews since their exodus began in the 1940s. That summer night, in the London garden lit up by hanging lights, we were happy. Michael made an inspiring speech about reactivating the time when there was harmony between faiths. His words were deeply moving for me – a Jew from Arab lands with happy childhood memories of life in Egypt. At fifteen, I had left to go to school in Paris, and from there moved to London to study art, but I kept going back to Egypt for holidays. Then suddenly, in 1956, after the Suez crisis, my parents and tens of thousands of fellow Jews were forced to flee their home in a hurry.

My parents joined me in London as refugees. For many years, we remained closely connected with relatives and friends from Egypt. A great number of them were passing through London on their way to a new homeland. Everyone talked about the foods they missed. We exchanged recipes – we might never see Egypt or each other again, but we would have something to remember each other by. There were no cookbooks and no printed recipes; dishes had been handed down in families. That is when I started collecting recipes. What I was collecting was a very mixed bag because Egypt had been a polyglot cosmopolitan society with many minorities living among the Muslim and Copt population. And the Jewish community itself was a mosaic of people from all over the old Ottoman lands and around the Mediterranean. My maternal grandmother was from Istanbul, and my other three grandparents came from Aleppo. Syrian refugees today are pining for the same dishes that my family longed for all those years ago.

Food becomes very important in exile. Families hold on to their dishes for generations, long after they have cast off their traditional clothes, dropped their native language, and stopped listening to their own forms of music. Michael's family fled Iraq for the United States in 1947 as a result of riots and reprisals against Jews. He has used cooking as a way of celebrating the family's origin and the harmony that once reigned between Jews and Muslims.

The Jews of Baghdad were the oldest community of the Jewish Diaspora. It was established in 586 BCE after the destruction of the First Temple, when the Babylonian monarch Nebuchadnezzar conquered Judea and deported much of the population to Babylon. When the exiles were allowed to return to the land of Israel fifty years later by the Persian king Cyrus, the majority decided to stay. Almost all the Jews of Iraq are descended from those brought as captives 2,500 years ago. Most lived in Baghdad, which had an enormous Jewish population. Other centres were in Mosul and Basra. The community was closely knit and traditional, and at the same time very integrated and rooted in society.

Many Iraqi-Jewish dishes can be traced back to when Baghdad was the capital of the Abbasid Caliphate in the Golden Age of Islam. When I was researching *The Book of Jewish Food*, I was amazed to find that family recipes given by friends from Iraq were strangely similar to ones in a thirteenth-century culinary manuscript found in Baghdad. One of the features of the old medieval Arab high style of cooking that derived from ancient Persia and was transported through north Africa as far as Spain was the mixing of sweet with sour and savoury with sweet, and date syrup was an important part of these flavour marriages.

Michael's Lamassu in Trafalgar Square made out of date syrup cans celebrates the old civilization as well as its cooking in a breathtakingly glorious way. And now *A House With A Date Palm Will Never Starve*, with its mix of traditional classics and modern innovative recipes created by some of our greatest chefs in Britain and America, brings us the flavour of a world when peoples lived together in harmony – with a twist.

Claudia Roden is an Egyptian-British cookbook writer and cultural anthropologist.

Introduction   Michael Rakowitz

'A house with a date palm will never starve.'
— Mesopotamian proverb

My grandfather, Nissim Isaac Daoud
bin Aziz, in the 1960s

The object as counter-historian
It is important to begin at the beginning. In 1947, my maternal
grandfather, Nissim Isaac Daoud bin Aziz, an Iraqi Jew, fled
Iraq with his family and came to the United States. They
settled in Great Neck, Long Island, and Nissim Isaac Daoud
bin Aziz became Nissim Isaac David. His business, Davisons
& Co., an import–export company that was among the most
successful in the Middle East, found a new home in New York
City. It closed in the 1960s. My grandfather died in 1975.

In August 2004, I discovered a large red can of date syrup
at Sahadi Importing Co., on Atlantic Avenue in Brooklyn.
Sahadi's was one of the stores my grandparents frequented
when they arrived in New York. When I brought the can to the
cash register, the owner Charlie Sahadi said, 'Your mother's
going to love this. It's from Baghdad.' I looked at the label,
which was clearly marked 'Product of Lebanon'. And that's
when he told me that the syrup was processed in the Iraqi
capital, put into large plastic vats, and driven over the border
into Syria, where it gets packed in unmarked cans. It then
crosses into Lebanon, gets a label, and is exported to the rest
of the world. From 1990 until May 2003, this was one method
that Iraqi companies used to circumvent UN sanctions. When
I asked why it was still being practised more than a year after
sanctions had ended, Charlie replied that prohibitive customs
and security charges were to blame. Importing directly from
Iraq was just too much of a risk. It would be bad business.

After this impromptu first lesson on importing, I decided
to further investigate the history of Iraqi exports. The
date syrup led me to dates, which were legendary in Iraq
and renowned as the best in the world, with more than six
hundred different varieties. In the 1970s, Iraq was the world's
chief exporter of dates, and dates accounted for its second

largest economy after oil. At its peak in the middle of that decade, the Iraqi date industry counted thirty million date palms in the country. By the end of the Iran–Iraq War in 1988, this number had been halved, to about sixteen million. At the end of the 2003 invasion, only three million remained.

Three years later, I reopened my grandfather's import–export company as a storefront on Atlantic Avenue in a venture called *Return*, presented by the innovative New York arts organization Creative Time. The project was conceived in part to shine a light on the logistical difficulties and roundabout methods of sending and receiving shipments from a country under foreign occupation and facing an uncertain future. A portion of the budget was allocated to provide free shipping for Iraqis living in the US (prices were exorbitant due to the deteriorating situation). The shop also addressed the absence of anything bearing the label 'Product of Iraq' on American store shelves, and the reopened business succeeded in signing the first contract in nearly thirty years to import one ton of world-famous Iraqi dates. The narrative of the dates' ill-fated journey to the US mirrored the plight of hundreds of thousands of Iraqi refugees as they waited in a line of traffic that was four days long at the Jordanian border, only to be sent back and forth to Baghdad, then finally to Damascus, where the Iraqi exporter determined that they had been spoiled. While ten new boxes of dates were airlifted out of Baghdad and into New York City in December 2006, the overall transaction served as a surrogate for a larger tragedy.

There are no Iraqi restaurants in New York
The veiled and absent products inspired another ongoing project, *Enemy Kitchen*. Though begun in spring 2003, this itinerant cooking workshop built upon a moment from January 1991, when I witnessed Iraq for the first time, in real time via CNN's green-tinted images – night vision. I saw buildings in Iraq that I would never visit being blown

A can exported from Lebanon but containing Iraqi date syrup

The storefront on Atlantic Avenue, Brooklyn, where I reopened Davisons & Co. in 2006

up by American bombs. There at the dinner table, watching all this unfold, I realized that the place my grandparents had fled to was destroying the place they had fled from. I felt bifurcated, fragmented. My mother saw how this was affecting me, and got my and my brothers' attention, distracting us from the television. 'Do you know there are no Iraqi restaurants in New York?' she said. It was like a riddle from the Sphinx. Later, I understood what she meant: that Iraq was not visible in this country beyond oil and war. Our whole history was under attack, and everything we knew about Iraq was suddenly a counter-history. I grew up hearing enchanted stories of the Iraqi capital from my grandmother: towers that 'sang the time' (minarets), scorpions in the basement, majestic date palms. My grandmother's stories were threatened, and in many ways, I have been working ever since to save them.

Serving from the *Enemy Kitchen* food truck in the plaza of the Museum of Contemporary Art, Chicago, in 2017

In the *Enemy Kitchen* workshop, I use Baghdadi recipes collected with my mother and teach them to different audiences. For one early incarnation, I cooked with a group of schoolkids from New York. Some had relatives in the US Army stationed in Iraq. In preparing and then consuming the food, it opened up another topic through which the word 'Iraq' could be discussed – in this case, attached to food, to culture, to shared humanity.

This cultural puncture, resulting from war, is one that I wanted to see happen on a larger scale. The invisibility in the United States of Iraqi culture, beyond the daily news, is alarming. Thus, in 2012, *Enemy Kitchen* evolved to become a functional food truck on the streets of Chicago that employs Iraqi refugee cooks, with US veterans of the Iraq War serving as their sous chefs. In this way, the power dynamic present in Iraq is inverted, as Americans now take orders from the Iraqis.

The time I spent on the food truck, witnessing the healing conversations between former soldiers and the citizens they once occupied or displaced, reminded me of my time in that storefront in Brooklyn, waiting for the Iraqi dates to arrive.

With a store open for three months without the main product, it left a lot of downtime. It was during these quiet moments that my attention was drawn to the labels and packaging of date syrup and date cookies that were products of Iraq but could not say that they were. It was like they were victims of xenophobia, forced to maintain a veiled provenance.

When you sit with an object long enough, it starts to tell you about itself, and what it wants to be
In December 2006, when I closed Davisons & Co., having sold the last imported date, I began *The invisible enemy should not exist*, a project that continues to this day. The title is a direct translation of *Aj-ibur-shapu*, the name of the ancient Babylonian processional way that ran through the Ishtar Gate. The centrepiece is an ongoing series of sculptures that attempt to reconstruct the seven thousand artefacts looted from the National Museum of Iraq in April 2003 during the Iraq War and those stolen and destroyed in its aftermath, mostly by ISIS. These life-size reconstructions are made from the packaging of Middle Eastern foodstuffs, including the wrappers of date cookies and cans of date syrup, as well as local Arabic newspapers – moments of cultural visibility found in cities across the US. The objects are created with assistants using the University of Chicago's Oriental Institute database and Interpol's website, which list each lost artefact with historical information, dimensions, and photographs.

   The majority of the artefacts reconstructed as part of *The invisible enemy should not exist* ranged in size from ancient cylinder seals that were the length of a small child's fingertip to votive statues that stood, at most, seventy-five centimetres tall. All that changed dramatically when I was invited to submit a proposal for the Fourth Plinth Commission in 2015. The empty Fourth Plinth in London's Trafalgar Square measures approximately four by two and a half metres (fourteen by eight feet). So too did the Lamassu, a winged-bull protective

One of the reconstructions of artefacts looted or destroyed during and since the Iraq War of 2003

The maquette proposal for the Fourth Plinth commission in 2015

deity that stood at the entrance to the Nergal Gate of Nineveh from around 700 BC until February 2015, when ISIS destroyed it, along with artefacts in the nearby Mosul Museum.

So when I won the commission to create a work for the plinth, I decided to reconstruct the lost Lamassu, using more than ten thousand empty cans of Iraqi date syrup as cladding over an underlying steel armature. As with all my projects, the cycle of materials – their provenance and their aura – is important. While the bronze elements of Nelson's Column are made from cannons salvaged from the wreck of the HMS *Royal George*, the salvage of date syrup cans makes present the human, economic, and ecological disasters caused by the various wars in Iraq and their aftermath. The reverse side of the sculpture features a carved cuneiform inscription originally concealed by being cemented to the wall of the Nergal Gate. Here, in the Lamassu's removed and displaced state, the cuneiform is exposed, proclaiming: 'Sennacherib, king of the world, king of Assyria, had the (inner) and outer wall of Nineveh built anew and raised as high as mountain(s).'

The reconstruction of the Lamassu allows an apparition to haunt Trafalgar Square at a time when we are witnessing a massive migration of people fleeing Iraq and Syria. I see the work as a ghost of the original, and as a placeholder for those human lives that cannot be reconstructed, that are still searching for sanctuary. Unlike the Lamassu housed inside the British Museum, my recreation stands outdoors with wings raised, still performing its duty as guardian of Iraq's past and present, hoping to return in the future.

With so many date syrup cans, a question arises: where did all that date syrup go?
This cookbook seeks to extend the space of the Lamassu, beyond the Fourth Plinth into your cupboards and bellies. It is a way to taste the sculpture. It brings together a cast of cooks – from diasporic Iraqis such as my mother, Yvonne Rakowitz,

The Lamassu on the Fourth Plinth in Trafalgar Square after it was unveiled in March 2018, with the National Gallery in the background

The reverse of the Lamassu with the inscription honouring Sennacherib, king of Assyria (740–681 BC)

Nawal Nasrallah, and Philip Juma to international chefs and food writers including Claudia Roden, Yotam Ottolenghi, Giorgio Locatelli, and Alice Waters – to collate traditional recipes and create new ones using date syrup.

In November 2018, *Enemy Kitchen* came to London. Collaborations with the charity Chefs in Schools took place at Gayhurst Community School in Hackney, where the children tried a traditional Iraqi breakfast of date syrup and tahini with flatbreads, and discussed where food comes from, using the Fourth Plinth as a starting point. I also joined a home economics lesson at Elizabeth Garrett Anderson School in Islington (*pp. 20–1*), cooking with date syrup to discuss the politics of food. Meanwhile, at Refettorio Felix in Earl's Court, a not-for-profit set up by the Italian chef Massimo Bottura, where the cooks had never tasted or used date syrup before, London-based chefs Philip Juma and Linda Dangoor (*opposite*) and I set ourselves the challenge of cooking with surplus food. The aim of Refettorio Felix is 'inclusion through food', and we served up a three-course lunch to more than sixty guests at their community kitchen, which is open to rough sleepers, homeless, and those on a low income.

We began with a proverb: 'A house with a date palm will never starve.' One might think it refers only to the fruit from this ubiquitous tree in the Mesopotamian landscape. But it is about all the palm's elements: the dates, the shade it provides, the fallen leaves for woven furniture, and finally, the wood that can be used to expand the house as the family grows. All these elements sustain life and the home. And so I hope what this sculpture began can be sustained. A sculpture that became a cookbook. A cookbook that will create a wider appreciation for date syrup. A wider appreciation for date syrup that will, *inshallah*, help replant those disappeared date palms.

In Iraq, it is traditional for parents to place a date in the mouth of their newborn baby, so its first taste of life is sweet: a harbinger of good things to come. Here's to a sweeter future.

The children at Gayhurst Community School in Hackney enjoyed the sweet delights of date syrup and tahini.

Refettorio Felix invites guest chefs from around the world to serve a three-course lunch to the most vulnerable in society.

Brunch

Philip Juma

Pancakes with clotted cream and Basra date syrup

200g / 2 cups plain flour
25g / 2 tbsp caster
 (castor) sugar
25g / ¼ cup milk powder
12g / 1 tbsp baking powder
5g / 1 tsp table salt
240ml / 1 cup milk, full fat
2 eggs
60g / ¼ cup butter, melted

To serve
Basra date syrup
 (as much as you like)
1 tbsp clotted cream

Serves 4

This is inspired by a classic Iraqi breakfast dish: *kahi*, layers of fluffy, flaky pastry, topped with *qemar*, a deliciously thick cream made from buffalo milk (see pages 176–7). My version uses pancakes instead. The recipe is just as amazing, and the pancakes are so light and fluffy because of the higher baking powder content. Anyone who tries them always asks for the recipe.

❧

Mix together all the dry ingredients and sift through a sieve into a mixing bowl.

In another large bowl, whisk the eggs and milk together. Gradually add the dry mix and keep whisking until your batter comes together. Be careful not to overmix! Mix the batter just enough to hydrate the dry ingredients, then stop.

Pour your melted butter into the batter and gently stir to incorporate.

With a dry non-stick pan, on a medium heat, spoon your pancake mix to your desired size. Do not move them once in the pan – let the heat do the work and, after a few minutes, you will see small bubbles forming on the surface. At this point, flip. Continue cooking until they are golden brown.

Pile three to five pancakes on a plate and pour the Basra date syrup all over them. Finish with a quenelle of clotted cream and devour while warm.

Philip Juma is an English-Irish-Iraqi food writer and founder and head chef of JUMA Kitchen in London.

Philip Juma

Bacon and date bites

20 strips pancetta
20 pieces of Iraqi dates
  (ideally) or firm dates
75ml / 5 tbsp Basra
  date syrup
10g / 1 tbsp sesame seeds

Serves 6

I love this recipe. It's simple and delicious. The sweetness from the dates complements the salty, fatty flavour of the bacon so well. It was originally a recipe I created for a canapé party, and then became a real favourite.

❉

Preheat the oven to 170 °C / 340 °F / gas mark 4.

Make a slit half way down each date to remove the stones, and then set aside.

Take the pancetta and lay out the strips vertically in front of you. Place a date at the bottom of the strip and roll upwards and away from you, encasing the date in the pancetta roll, and repeat.

Arrange all the pieces on a baking tray and place in the oven for 15–20 minutes. You are looking for the fat to have melted and the dates to have become sticky.

While warm, drizzle over the Basra date syrup and sprinkle over the sesame seeds for a light crunch.

Philip Juma is an English-Irish-Iraqi food writer and founder and head chef of JUMA Kitchen in London.

Shatha Alimara Najib

Iraqi-inspired eggs with date syrup

3 tbsp olive oil
1 small red onion
 (sliced thinly)
2 eggs
1 tbsp date syrup
½ tsp salt

Serves 1

If you have ever had maple syrup with your eggs, you will understand why this is a popular dish in the Middle East. Nutritious and high in fibre, it can be served with *samoon*, Iraqi sourdough flatbread, for breakfast or with greens for a filling lunch. Halve the quantity of date syrup or double the eggs if you like it less sweet.

In a pan over a medium heat, fry the onion with olive oil until it is caramelized. Meanwhile, beat the eggs with salt and date syrup. Add the egg mixture to the pan, whisking for one minute until ready. Turn off the heat and enjoy immediately.

Shatha Alimara Najib is a London-based Iraqi cook and YouTuber.

Reem Kassis

Tahini and molasses spread

90g / ¼ cup tahini
90g / ¼ cup grape
   molasses or date syrup
Pitta (pita) bread,
   homemade or
   store-bought, to serve

Serves 2

Whenever my father had to go to Hebron for a work meeting in the summer, my mother would insist he bring back the grape molasses the town is so famous for. While the molasses can be used the same way one would use honey or maple syrup, we use it mostly for making this richly flavoured *dibis wa tahini* spread. In Iraq, they use date syrup instead of grape molasses and it is known as *dibis wa rashi*.

Pour the tahini into a small, shallow bowl. Drizzle the molasses in a nice pattern over the tahini.

Serve with warm pitta bread. Mix together just before eating or use your bread to mix as you eat.

While I use a ratio of tahini to molasses or syrup of 1:1, you can adjust to suit your taste with more or less molasses. If you cannot find grape molasses or date syrup, honey is an excellent alternative. This spread will keep well at room temperature, covered in plastic wrap, for a day or two.

Reem Kassis is a Palestinian
writer and cookbook author
based in Philadelphia.

Prue Leith

Bananas on brioche toast with date syrup

Butter for frying
2 small bananas,
  split lengthwise
2 thick slices brioche
1 tbsp rum
2 tbsp date syrup
20g / 2 tbsp hazelnuts,
  toasted
2 scoops vanilla
  ice cream

Serves 2

This is a deliciously bad-for-you dish. For birthdays only.

Heat a teaspoon of butter in a frying pan until foaming. Fry the bananas fairly fast, flat side down, to brown them on that side only. Remove the slices from the pan. Heat some more butter (a good tablespoon) and fry the brioche on both sides. Put each slice on a plate and top with the bananas. Mix the rum with the date syrup and drizzle over. Sprinkle with the hazelnuts and add a scoop of ice cream to each plate.

Prue Leith is a British-South African restaurateur, chef, broadcaster, writer, and founder of Leiths School of Food and Wine and catering company Leith's Dining.

Jeremy Lee

Granola with yoghurt and date syrup

200g / 1½ cups
  sunflower seeds
260g / 2 cups almonds,
  coarsely chopped
230g / 2 cups walnuts,
  coarsely chopped
150g / 1 cup cashews,
  coarsely chopped
150g / 1 cup raw
  sesame seeds
90g / 1 cup raw wheatgerm
500g / 6 cups rolled oats
340g / 1 cup honey
230ml / 1 cup oil
Greek yoghurt, to serve
Date syrup, to serve

This is a recipe from the American artist Georgia O'Keeffe, which we have used for many years to make the granola we serve for breakfast at Quo Vadis. Topped with yoghurt and drizzled with date syrup, it is a fine way to start any morning.

Preheat the oven to 180 °C / 350 °F / gas mark 4 and mix the dry ingredients in a large bowl. Slowly heat the honey and oil until it is smooth and runny, add to the bowl, and stir until well combined. Spread the granola mixture between two oiled baking trays and place them in the oven, turning often until lightly browned on all sides. Cool the granola to room temperature, then store in airtight containers. Once cooled and ready to serve, top with yoghurt and a drizzle of date syrup.

Jeremy Lee is a British food
broadcaster and chef-proprietor
at Quo Vadis, London.

Salads, Sides, and Dips

Anna Jones

Figs with sticky date dressing

For the dressing
1 shallot, peeled and very
  finely chopped
½ tsp Dijon mustard
1 tbsp date syrup
  (or 2 dates blitzed
  with a little oil)
Juice of 1 lemon
Sea salt and freshly
  ground black pepper
2 tbsp extra virgin olive oil
1 small bunch of fresh mint

For the salad
8 big handfuls of
  mixed salad leaves
  (I use rocket, radicchio,
  baby chard, and
  mustard greens)
6 fresh figs, quartered
1 small bunch of fresh basil
100g / ¾ cup soft goat's
  cheese or goat's curd

Serves 4

This is a killer dressing for any robust salad. If figs are not in season, peaches, thinly sliced apples, or clementines are all good too. I use date syrup here – it's a great, completely natural sugar with a wonderful deep, malty back note. Otherwise, a couple of dates blitzed with a little oil will work, as will some good thick balsamic vinegar.

Put the chopped shallot, mustard, date syrup, and lemon juice into a jug. Season with salt and pepper and drizzle in the oil, whisking as you go. Chop the mint, add to the jug, and set aside.

Put the salad leaves into a bowl and scatter the figs over. Give the dressing a good mix, then drizzle it over the salad. Pick the basil leaves off the stems and scatter over the salad, then toss everything together.

Dot the goat's cheese over the top and it's ready to serve.

Anna Jones is a British cook,
stylist, and writer known for her
focus on vegetarian food.

Shatha Alimara Najib

Figs with date syrup salad

1 can (drained weight
220g / 1½ cups) hearts
of palm, each sliced
into 4 pieces
4 figs, each sliced
into 4 pieces
90g / ½ cup spinach
45g / ¼ cup radish
2 medium-sized cucumbers
(approx. 110g / ¾ cup)
1 small red onion
30g / ¼ cup walnuts

For the dressing
1 tbsp date syrup
2 tbsp olive oil
1 tbsp balsamic vinegar
½ tsp salt

Serves 2–3

The praises of dates and figs are continually sung in the Middle East: dates are the 'fruits of paradise', while figs are the 'one fruit to rule them all'. This salad is for those days when you would like a light, Middle Eastern-inspired meal. Pine nuts can replace walnuts, and avocados can be added for a more substantial dish. Think of the recipe as a foundation on which you can build.

Wash the spinach and dry it well. Finely slice the cucumbers, radish, and onion and add them to the spinach in a bowl. Add the sliced figs and palm hearts; wash the walnuts and add them to the bowl. Mix the date syrup, olive oil, balsamic vinegar, and salt for a dressing, drizzle onto the salad, and serve.

Shatha Alimara Najib is a London-based Iraqi cook and YouTuber.

Reem Kassis

Aubergine, yoghurt, and nut salad

1kg / 2lb 2oz
 (about 4 medium)
 aubergines (eggplants)
Olive oil, for brushing
Salt and black pepper

For the yoghurt sauce
400g / 14oz Greek yoghurt
1 small garlic clove, crushed
½ tsp salt
1 tsp lemon juice

For the garnish
2 tbsp pomegranate seeds
50g / ½ cup lightly toasted
 mixed nuts, such as pine
 nuts, almonds, pistachios,
 cashews, or hazelnuts
1 small handful of green
 leaves, such as rocket
 (arugula), dill, or chives
2 tbsp date syrup

Serves 4–6

Whenever we invited people over for a big lunch, my mother would make a variation of this salad – always the highlight for me. I have adapted it into something that we eat at home on a weekly basis; the date syrup drizzled on top is a wonderful contrast to the sharp yoghurt and a perfect companion to the crunchy nuts.

Preheat the grill (broiler) to high. Slice the aubergines into 1.5-cm (¾-inch) rounds, brush both sides with olive oil, and sprinkle with salt and pepper. Place the aubergines on an oven rack and grill (broil) for about ten minutes on each side, or until they develop a golden brown exterior.

Meanwhile, put all the ingredients for the yoghurt sauce into a bowl and whisk together to a smooth consistency.

Once the aubergines are done, arrange in overlapping circles on a round platter. Spoon over the yoghurt mixture then top with pomegranate seeds, toasted nuts, and green leaves. Drizzle the date syrup on top and serve.

As a variation, use courgettes (zucchini), cut in half and sliced lengthwise, instead of the aubergines, and use walnuts, pomegranate seeds, and sumac for the garnish.

Reem Kassis is a Palestinian
writer and cookbook author
based in Philadelphia.

Nuno Mendes

Fennel salad

3 heads of fennel
3 tbsp date syrup
Extra virgin olive oil
1 bunch of chives, chopped
Maldon salt

This simple yet delicious fennel salad is a perfect aromatic accompaniment to a variety of fish mains, especially oven-baked salmon recipes.

Shave the fennel heads very thinly and season with Maldon salt, extra virgin olive oil, chopped chives, and three heaping tablespoons of date syrup. Serve on the side or on top of the salmon dish on pages 104–5.

Nuno Mendes, originally from Portugal, is the executive chef at Chiltern Firehouse and Mãos in London.

Linda Dangoor

Aubergine salad and beetroot salad

Aubergine salad
2 or 3 aubergines
 (eggplants)

For the dressing
3 tbsp tahini
4 tbsp lemon juice
4 tbsp water
3 tbsp extra virgin olive oil
2 garlic cloves, crushed or
 minced very finely
4 tbsp yoghurt (optional)
½ tsp salt or to taste
½ tsp cayenne pepper
 or to taste
Pepper to taste

Serves 3–4

Beetroot salad
4 medium-sized beetroots
Juice of 1 lemon
3 tbsp olive oil
Salt and pepper to taste
Flat-leaf parsley, finely
 chopped for the garnish

Serves 4

The three salads here can accompany the mains in this book as sides or be eaten on their own. The buttery texture and smoky flavour of the charred aubergine give a truly distinctive taste to the salad below. The tahini adds an amazing taste to the dish. For the *zalatat shwander* (beetroot salad), I usually bake the beetroots, but you can also steam them.

Wash the aubergines and prick them all over with a fork. This will stop them from bursting. Chargrill the skin of the aubergine directly in the flame of the stove until it turns black. You can also do this by grilling (broiling) in the oven, although it will take a little longer, about forty minutes.

Allow to cool sufficiently to peel off the skin, and then top and tail each aubergine. The insides should be quite soft.

Cut into cubes of about two centimetres (one inch). Arrange on a serving dish. Mix the dressing ingredients into a creamy paste and pour over the warm aubergine.

Preheat the oven to 190°C / 375°F / gas mark 5.

Wash the beetroots thoroughly. Wrap each one in foil. Place them on a baking tray and bake for about an hour. When cooked, unwrap and allow to cool.

Peel and slice the beetroots. Do not slice them before they are cooked as their juice will seep out. Arrange them in a dish, add the lemon juice and parsley, and season with salt and pepper. Drizzle with olive oil.

You can cut the beetroots into cubes, and use the dressing as above with a tablespoon or two of chopped fresh ginger.

Linda Dangoor

Chickpea salad

250g / 1¼ cups dried
  chickpeas, soaked overnight
1 fresh tomato, finely
  chopped
1 handful of finely chopped
  fresh coriander (cilantro)
¼ tsp bicarbonate of soda,
  to help soften the peas

For the dressing
½ a preserved lemon,
  finely chopped
1 garlic clove, crushed
4 tbsp lemon juice
6 tbsp extra virgin olive oil
½ tsp salt or to taste
¼ tsp cayenne pepper

Serves 4 or more

These peas are a street food we call *lablabi*. The street vendors in Baghdad used to shout '*Lablabi!*' at every corner. Ali, the local chickpea seller, used to park his trolley outside our school every afternoon and wait for the hungry pupils to spill out. When our lessons were over, he was mobbed. I can still picture him dishing out piping-hot chickpeas into tiny bowls, sprinkling them with salt before handing them over to us. We would eat them on the hop before going home. In this recipe, I have added a spicy dressing with cayenne pepper, combined with some preserved lemon (which gives it a very distinctive taste) and fresh coriander (cilantro), making an intensely flavoured salad out of this humble legume. If you do not have preserved lemons, you can add the zest of a lemon instead.

Drain the soaked chickpeas and place in a saucepan. Cover with water, add the bicarbonate of soda, and bring to the boil. Turn down to a medium heat, half cover and cook for about 1 hour 15 minutes. The peas should be soft but not mushy. Drain and leave aside to cool down.

Meanwhile, mix the dressing ingredients in a salad bowl. Combine the cooled chickpeas with the dressing and combine well. At this point, taste and adjust the seasoning and tartness.

Add the tomatoes and chopped coriander (or parsley if preferred), and give the whole salad a good mix.

Linda Dangoor is an Iraqi artist and
food writer based in London.

Caroline Eden

Beetroot and dill dip

250g / 1⅔ cups whole, unpeeled raw beetroot
½ a garlic clove, crushed
2 tbsp lemon juice
2 tbsp fresh dill, chopped
1 generous pinch of sea salt flakes
3 tbsp sour cream
2 tbsp date syrup

Serves 4 (generously)

This is an easy dip to make, inspired by the flavours of the Caucasus. It works well as an appetizer, a side dish, or with breadsticks, crackers, and pitta (pita) bread.

Preheat the oven to 220 °C / 425 °F / gas mark 7.

Wrap the beetroot in foil and roast until a skewer easily pierces the flesh. This can take forty-five minutes to an hour, maybe a little longer, depending on the size of the beetroot. Allow to cool, then peel. Roughly chop the beetroot and put it in a food processor with the garlic, lemon, dill, and salt, and blitz until smooth, pausing occasionally to scrape down the sides to help it on its way. Tip the beetroot mixture into a serving bowl and stir in the cream and syrup. Taste and adjust the seasoning. Serve at room temperature, perhaps with a dill sprig or two to decorate.

Caroline Eden is a British food and travel writer focusing on the countries of the former Soviet Union and south Asia.

Yvonne Rakowitz

Iraqi charoset

Date syrup
Chopped walnuts
 or pecans

Date syrup, known among the Jews of Baghdad as *silan*, can be used the same way that one uses honey. It is one of the two ingredients of the Iraqi version of charoset, a sweet, dark paste eaten at Passover. Its colour and texture symbolize the clay used by the Israelites during their bondage in Egypt. Some Jewish traditions make it from a mixture of fruits, nuts, spices, and even sweet red wine, but this is a simpler version.

Yvonne Rakowitz, the mother of Iraqi-American artist Michael Rakowitz, has worked with her son to preserve and pass on her family's Iraqi culture and traditional cooking.

In individual small bowls, pour enough date syrup to half-fill each one. Top with a generous serving of chopped nuts.

Rosie Sykes

Cashew nut carrots

360g / 2½ cups carrots
120g / ¾ cup cashew nuts
3 garlic cloves, peeled
 and crushed
1 small handful of parsley
1 tbsp olive oil

This cashew mixture will keep well in the fridge and can work like a pesto. It should be served with the spiced duck glazed with date syrup on pages 138–9. It will also go well with any vegetable as an accompaniment or tossed through some pasta.

Put the garlic, nuts, and parsley in a food processor and whizz to a rough mix. Add the olive oil, salt, and pepper. Steam the carrots and toss with a couple of generous spoonfuls of the cashew mixture.

Rosie Sykes is a British chef and food writer.

SALADS, SIDES, AND DIPS   53

Reem Kassis

Muhamarra

150g / 5oz (about 1 large)
  roasted red bell pepper
  (see method)
4 tbsp olive oil, plus
  extra for drizzling
4 tbsp pomegranate
  molasses (no added sugar)
1 or 2 tbsp date syrup
1 tbsp tahini
2 tsp chilli powder
  (see method)
1 tsp paprika
¼ tsp ground cumin
¼ tsp salt
¼ tsp finely ground coffee
  (optional, see method)
150g / 1½ cups
  walnut pieces, plus extra
  for garnish
25g / ½ cup breadcrumbs

Serves 6–8 as part
  of a mezze spread

In the late 1800s, my great-great-grandmother moved to Palestine from Syria as a bride. Along with her beautiful bridal trunk, she brought many of her family's recipes, among them muhamarra. Sweet and tart, crunchy and smooth, this classic Levantine dip is perfect on its own, with bread, and even as a sauce with grilled meats.

You can roast your own bell peppers at home, but I tend to use the jarred variety for convenience. Just make sure there are no flavourings or additives, and that they are preserved in vinegar and water, not oil.

The dip is supposed to be spicy, but you can adjust to your taste. If you reduce the amount of chilli, then increase the paprika by the same amount to retain the nice red colour.

As for the coffee, my great-great-grandmother used to say that it helped bring all the flavours together, but it is an addition that can easily be left out.

Put all the ingredients, except the walnuts and breadcrumbs, into the bowl of a food processor and process until smooth. Add the walnuts and breadcrumbs and pulse until the walnuts are coarsely chopped. You want this dip to retain some texture and not be entirely smooth, so do not overpulse.

Transfer the dip to a bowl and mix with a spoon to combine. To serve, spread in a platter, drizzle with olive oil, and garnish with walnuts.

Reem Kassis is a Palestinian
writer and cookbook author
based in Philadelphia.

Vegetables

Anna Jones

Bay, date, and saffron-roasted cauliflower

2 pinches of saffron strands
1 large or 2 small
  cauliflowers (approx.
  1kg / 2lb 4oz), leaves
  clicked off, head broken
  into medium florets,
  stalk roughly chopped
2 medium onions, peeled
  and finely sliced
1 tbsp Turkish chilli
  flakes or 1 good pinch
  of dried chilli flakes
3 bay leaves
Sea salt and freshly
  ground black pepper
1 tbsp date syrup
1 handful of raisins
  (I use golden ones)
1 handful of almonds,
  roughly chopped
1 bunch of fresh parsley,
  roughly chopped

Serves 4

I usually turn to Indian spices when I think of cauliflower, but one bright May Day I chose instead the sunshine warmth of saffron and the mellow back note of bay. I throw in a handful of golden raisins and top with a little date syrup for some sweetness and almonds for crunch.

Preheat the oven to 200°C / 400°F (fan 180°C / 350°F / gas mark 6).

Put the saffron into a little bowl, cover it with a couple of teaspoons of boiling water, and leave it to steep. Get a large, deep baking tray, throw in the cauliflower, onions, chilli flakes, and bay leaves, and season with salt and pepper. Once the saffron has steeped, pour in the saffron strands and their liquid, add the raisins, date syrup, and almonds, toss everything together, then cover with foil and bake in the oven for twenty minutes.

Remove the foil and bake for a further ten to fifteen minutes, until the tips are burnished and the cauliflower is tender to the bite. Toss through the chopped parsley and serve.

Anna Jones is a British cook,
stylist, and writer known for
her focus on vegetarian food.

Olia Hercules

Turshulash-style roots and beans

250g / 1½ cups celeriac, peeled and diced

2 beetroots, peeled and diced small

2 quinces, peeled and diced small

250g / 1½ cups squash, peeled and diced

150g / 1½ cups okra

100g / ⅝ cup cooked chickpeas (the ones in a jar are the best)

2 tbsp good-quality vegetable oil

3 tbsp tomato paste

2 tbsp date syrup

Juice of 1 lemon or 60ml / 2fl oz verjuice

5g / ¼oz fresh oregano or marjoram, leaves picked

1 handful of chopped mint

Serves 4–6

I love it when traditional recipes inspire or have a slight makeover. Turshulash – meaning 'sour dinner' – is usually a gorgeous seven-bean, carrot, and beetroot dish from Lenkaran, in southern Azerbaijan. My friend Zulfiya's mother comes from there. This is her version of the dish, slightly adapted by me.

Put the celeriac, quince, and squash in a pan with just enough cold water to cover. Bring it to a simmer and cook for ten minutes, uncovered.

Heat the oil and tomato paste and cook for a few minutes while stirring. Add the okra and beetroot, cooking for five minutes over a medium heat. Add the date syrup and the lemon juice, and then incorporate the mixture into the celeriac pot along with the oregano or marjoram.

Finally, add the chickpeas and cook for another five to ten minutes. Switch the heat off, cover the pan with a lid, and leave to stand for half an hour or so. Serve with fresh mint.

Olia Hercules is a London-based Ukrainian chef, food writer, and food stylist.

Summer Thomas

Shalgham
Turnip stew with Basra date syrup

500g / 2¼ cups lamb
pieces on the bone
450g / 3 cups turnips,
peeled and quartered
1 can (400g / 2 cups)
chopped tomatoes
1 tbsp tomato purée
150g / 7 tbsp Basra
date syrup
5 garlic cloves,
each cut in half
3 tbsp brown sugar
5 tbsp lemon juice
2 tbsp dried mint
Water
Salt to taste

Serves 4

This beautiful dish is rarely found in Iraqi households these days, but it's one of my favourites. In our house, we fight over the bones to get the marrow, so we always add extra meat – it's the best part! The stew has a sweetness from the date syrup, with a delicate hint of sourness and fragrance from the mint. It is best served with fluffy white rice.

Put the lamb in a medium, heavy-based pot and cover with cold water and bring to the boil. You will see impurities rise to the top – rinse under water until they have all been washed away. Return the lamb to the pot and cover again with cold water. Bring to the boil, allowing the water to evaporate (thirty to forty minutes).

Meanwhile, combine the chopped tomatoes with purée and blend until completely smooth. Peel and chop the turnips. Add the date syrup to the lamb. When it starts to bubble, add the turnips, garlic, and tomato mix to the pot. Bring to a boil and add boiling water until all the ingredients are completely covered. When it is at a rolling boil, reduce the heat and leave the stew to simmer for twenty minutes.

Add sugar, lemon juice, and mint (and a cup of boiling water if the stew is reduced too much), continuing to simmer for another fifteen minutes. The lamb and turnips should be fully cooked now. Add salt to taste, and serve hot with rice.

Summer Thomas is an Iraqi-
British chef based in London.

Linda Dangoor

Shalgham helu
Sweet stewed turnips

8 medium turnips
4 tbsp date syrup
1 pinch of salt

Serves 4

We would buy turnips on the way home from school in Baghdad – such a basic street food, but absolutely delicious! I remember young and old men with their carts, turnips steaming, and going to buy one to eat there and then. You can make these turnips as sweet as you want – it's not a dessert, but it does taste sweet.

Wash the turnips and top and tail them. Do not peel.

Place the turnips in a large saucepan, add cold water to just cover them and a pinch of salt. Bring to the boil and continue boiling for about fifteen minutes. Add the date syrup and let it mix well in the water by moving the pot from side to side. Place a plate on top of the turnips to weigh them down. Cover and continue cooking on a medium heat for twenty-five minutes.

Preheat the oven to 150 °C / 300 °F / gas mark 2. You can either continue to cook in the pan for another thirty to forty minutes on a low heat (placing a heat diffuser under the pot to stop the bottom from burning) or transfer the turnips to an ovenproof dish with a lid. If you choose to do the latter, pour in the liquid to half cover the turnips. Bake, covered for one hour or more. The turnips will turn brown and their taste will be richer.

Serve hot and eat as is.

Linda Dangoor is an Iraqi artist and food writer based in London.

Linda Dangoor

Bamia hameth
Sweet-and-sour okra

400g / 4 cups frozen
  baby okra

For the sauce
1 large onion, finely chopped
400g / 2 cups tomatoes,
  fresh or canned, chopped
350ml / 12fl oz water
1 tbsp tomato paste
2 to 3 garlic cloves, peeled
Juice of 2½ lemons
Juice of ½ orange
1 tbsp pomegranate or
  date syrup (optional)
1 pinch of vegetable stock
  cube or bouillon powder
2 tbsp sugar or to taste
Salt and pepper to taste

Serves 4–5

Okra, or *bamia* in Arabic, is a summer vegetable with a short season. My grandmothers used to thread them on a string like a necklace and dry them in the sun, cooking them in the winter or spring months. I prefer to use frozen ones: they are smaller, daintier, and do not require cleaning. If using fresh, remember to cook them longer.

Sauté the chopped onion in olive oil on a medium heat until soft and golden. Add the tomatoes and stir to mix. Cover and simmer on a low heat for about fifteen minutes or so, stirring occasionally. Do this until the tomatoes begin to melt. Add the tomato paste, the garlic, the pinch of vegetable stock, water, salt and pepper, and bring to the boil. Continue a gentle boil for ten minutes.

Add the frozen okra, bring back to the boil, and turn the heat down to a simmer. Cook for between fifteen and twenty-five minutes, depending on whether you like the okra soft or a little al dente.

Add the lemon and orange juice, syrup, and sugar, and mix well. Taste and adjust the sweet and sour flavour. Simmer for another five to ten minutes.

Serve hot with rice or bread.

Linda Dangoor is an Iraqi artist
and food writer based in London.

Russell Norman

Roasted Brussels sprouts with pancetta and date syrup

650g / 6 cups Brussels
  sprouts, trimmed and cut
  in half lengthways
200g / 1 cup pancetta,
  cut into small cubes
1 garlic clove,
  very finely chopped
3 tbsp extra virgin olive oil
2 tbsp date syrup
1 tbsp lemon juice
Flaky sea salt
Ground black pepper

Serves 4

A tasty alternative to plain steamed veggies, this is a delicious way to spice up your Sunday roast or a great side dish to serve as part of a feast.

Preheat the oven to 220°C / 425°F / gas mark 7.

Put the sprouts, garlic, olive oil, date syrup, and lemon juice into a large baking tray with deep sides. Toss several times until the sprouts are fully coated. Add a generous few pinches of sea salt and a good couple of twists of black pepper. Place in the oven for fifteen minutes.

Remove the tray (but leave the oven on) and scatter over the pancetta cubes. Toss all the ingredients once more and return to the oven for another ten to fifteen minutes until the edges of the cut sprouts are beginning to char and crisp and the pancetta has turned golden brown.

Serve immediately.

Russell Norman is a British
restaurateur and food writer.

Sara Leana Ahmad

Iraqi onion dolma

4–5 large onions
300g / 1½ cup basmati rice
450g / 1lb ground lamb
  or beef
20g / ½ cup or one bundle
  parsley, finely chopped
3 tbsp tomato paste
1 tbsp sea salt
1 tbsp sumac
Zest of 1 kaffir lime
90g / ¼ cup date syrup
2 tbsp olive oil

Serves 4–8

The stuffed onion dolma is often overlooked for the more spectacular aubergine or courgette versions, but everything falls apart without it. Inspired by how the onion at the bottom of the dolma pot often caramelizes a little, I have added date syrup to extend that hint of sweetness and texture. The kaffir lime zest in the stuffing lends some glamour.

Fill a medium stockpot a little over halfway with water and salt and bring to a boil. Peel the onions, cut off the tops and bottoms, and then make a cut halfway through each one from top to the bottom. Boil for about ten to fifteen minutes. Place the onions in a cold water bath and separate each layer, keeping the outer five or six.

Combine the rice, meat, parsley, tomato paste, sea salt, sumac, and zest. In a small bowl, combine the date syrup and oil. Spread a tablespoon of this mixture at the bottom of a non-stick medium pan. Stuff each onion layer with the rice mixture and place at the bottom of the pan, following the curve of the pot. Continue until at least a quarter of the pan is left free.

Add water to the pan to sit just above the dolma. Add the remaining date syrup mixture, shaking to incorporate. Now place a small plate upside down over the dolma and press down so the water rises up above the onions. Cover the pot and bring to a boil. Boil for twenty-five minutes before reducing to a simmer. Leave covered for at least forty minutes, the longer the better.

When ready to serve, carefully remove the plate from the top of the dolma. Place a large serving platter over the pot – it should be double the diameter of the pot. And then, *mashallah*, make a wish and flip the dolma pot tightly over the platter.

Sara Leana Ahmad is an Iraqi-American food blogger at Add a Little Lemon.

Sara Leana Ahmad

Vegan Iraqi dolma
Stuffed vegetables and vine leaves

2–3 onions
10–12 baby bell peppers
  (red or green)
2–3 small tomatoes
4–6 baby aubergines
  (eggplants)
4 small courgettes (zucchini)
10–12 vine (grape) leaves

For the stuffing
850g / 4 cups white
  basmati rice
8 medium tomatoes,
  coarsely chopped
2 bunches of flat-leaf parsley,
  coarsely chopped
3 garlic cloves
85g / ⅓ cup tomato paste
  (a little more or less is fine)
Approx. 100g / ⅓ cup date
  syrup (or more, to taste)
Approx. 120ml / ½ cup
  lemon juice
A dash of extra virgin olive oil
Sumac, quite a bit
Salt, to taste

For the broth
Water
360ml / 1½ cups lemon juice

Serves 4–8, depending on
  the company you keep

In this vegan version of the Iraqi dolma recipe, I stuff and roll onions, tomatoes, aubergine (eggplant), courgette (zucchini), bell peppers, and vine (grape) leaves with a classic filling minus the traditional meat. The date syrup accompanies the sour flavours in the stuffing and the broth with something sweet. Make this when you want to impress all your friends.

❊

Rinse and soak the rice for at least thirty minutes.

Meanwhile prepare the vegetables to be stuffed. First peel the onions and make a slit length-wise less than halfway through (make sure not go through the centre). Place the onions in a microwave-safe bowl and microwave for no more than two minutes; alternatively you can boil the onions until a little tender. Rush them to a cold water bath, and carefully take off the first four or five layers of each onion and put aside to be stuffed; save the rest of the onion for the stuffing in a bowl. Slice the tops off your peppers and rinse the inside to make sure there are no seeds. Slice the tops off the tomatoes and save them (tomatoes need their hats). Remove the insides carefully and save for the stuffing. Slice the tops off the aubergines (eggplants) and courgettes (zucchini), and cut them in half (if necessary). Remove and save the insides. Separate your vine (grape) leaves and keep in a cold water bath.

To make the stuffing, work the chopped tomato, parsley, garlic, and the removed contents of your cored vegetables in a food processor. Drain the rice well and mix the stuffing into the rice. Add the tomato paste, date syrup, lemon juice, and olive oil to the rice and mix. Add generous amounts of sumac and salt to taste. Mix again.

Arrange your station so you have an empty cooking pot to your left, a bowl with the stuffing in front of you, a bowl of cored vegetables to your right, and a small bowl of vine (grape) leaves.

Add a thin layer of olive oil to the bottom of your cooking pot. Begin by stuffing the onions, adding them to the bottom of the pot, and then move on to the aubergine (eggplant) and courgette (zucchini), peppers, and finally the tomatoes.

Now for the leaves. With the leaf flat, stem side up and stem removed, place a small portion of stuffing just about the stem line, tightly roll over, then fold both sides very tightly, and fold those edges again and flatten, and then roll the rest of the leaf tightly. Repeat, adding to the pot, and press everything firmly down.

Take the pot to the stove. Add a mixture of water and lemon juice to the pot so that when you press the vegetables down firmly, the water barely covers the vegetables. Place a dinner plate downwards on the vegetables, and cover with the pot lid.

Bring to a boil for about five minutes, and then simmer on low for about forty minutes. Remove lid and plate; if there is still liquid in the pot, carefully drain.

To serve, place a large serving plate on top of the pot and carefully flip the dolma onto the plate.

Sara Leana Ahmad is an Iraqi-American food blogger at Add a Little Lemon.

Philip Juma

Pumpkin soup with date syrup

1 large pumpkin
1 butternut squash
1 onion
2 carrots
2 celery stalks
4 garlic cloves
1.5l / 50fl oz
   vegetable stock
1 tsp turmeric
½ tsp cumin
½ tsp coriander
5 tbsp date syrup
400g / 6¾ cups
   wild mushroom
1 bunch of flat-leaf parsley
Pea shoots (optional)

Serves 10

I created this recipe when Michael asked me to cook with him at Refettorio Felix. It was an absolute privilege, although I had no idea what we were going to cook, a daunting, yet exciting prospect. When the delivery van arrived, I could see a beautiful range of pumpkins and squash. Immediately, I thought the combination of squash and date syrup would work, and the garlic mushroom garnish made it all the more special.

Preheat the oven to 190 °C / 375 °F / gas mark 5.

Peel the squash and pumpkin and cut into chunks. Toss in olive oil, salt, and pepper and roast for twenty minutes until soft with some colour.

While they are roasting, prepare the soup base. Peel the carrots and finely dice with the onion and celery. Sauté in a large saucepan with a glug of olive oil. Season with salt. Once they are translucent (after eight minutes), grate the garlic and add most of it to the pan, keeping back half a teaspoon. Stir in the garlic with the spices. After two minutes, take off the heat.

By now, the squash and pumpkin should be ready. Place the chunks into the pan and add the stock. Bring back to a medium heat. After five minutes, the chunks should be falling apart. If so, blitz the soup using a hand blender. Simmer on a low heat. Once puréed, add the date syrup. Add three tablespoons at first; add more depending on how sweet you like it.

In a separate pan, sauté the mushrooms in some olive oil on a high heat. Season with salt at the beginning, to extract the water. Once they have colour, add the remaining garlic and a handful of chopped parsley. Set aside.

To serve, ladle your soup into a small bowl. Garnish with mushrooms, parsley or pea shoots, and a drizzle of olive oil.

Philip Juma is an English-Irish-Iraqi food writer and founder and head chef of JUMA Kitchen in London.

Sam and Sam Clark

Fried aubergines with date syrup and whipped feta

2 aubergines (eggplants),
  cut into chunky chips
150ml / ⅔ cup olive oil
150ml / ⅔ cup sunflower oil
5 tbsp plain flour and 5 tbsp
  polenta, mixed together
  and seasoned with fine salt
3–4 tbsp date syrup
120g / ⅘ cup feta, blitzed
  with 2 tbsp of water and
  1 tsp of olive oil to a
  creamlike consistency
2 tbsp chopped fresh mint

Serves 4

For European chefs, the date represents the most romantic food of the east. It is the life giver of the desert. In its molasses form, it gives all its nutritional wonders combined with complex caramel notes and a dreamy texture.

Place the aubergine chips in a colander, toss with a teaspoon of fine sea salt and leave for thirty minutes to get rid of excess water and bitterness. Dry the aubergines well on kitchen paper. Heat both oils in a wide frying pan, until hot but not smoking (about 180°C / 350°F). Toss the aubergines in the seasoned flour and shake off any excess. Add the chips in a single layer (in batches if necessary) and fry until golden brown and crisp. Remove from the pan and place on kitchen paper to absorb any excess oil. Serve immediately with the whipped feta and date syrup drizzled all over, followed by the fresh mint.

Sam and Sam Clark are British restaurateurs, founders of Moro and Morito in London.

Rice and Grains

Sara Leana Ahmad

Dibis maqluba

300g / 1½ cups basmati
  rice, soaked and strained
1000ml / 4 cups water,
  for boiling
4 tbsp salt
  (3 for boiling, 1 for taste)
½ large onion, diced
2–3 garlic cloves, minced
3 tbsp tomato paste
60ml / ¼ cup vegetable broth
1 tomato, diced
Juice of ½ lemon
175g / ½ cup date syrup
2 tbsp olive oil
1 tsp salt
1 large aubergine, cut in
  1cm / ½in rounds
½ large onion, sliced
2 bell peppers, sliced
2 tomatoes, 1cm / ½in slices
350ml / 1½ cups oil
  for sautéing
20g / ½ cup parsley,
  finely chopped

Serves 4–6

Maqluba is a dish to prepare when you have guests. It literally means 'upside down', and is a layered rice dish that you triumphantly finish by flipping upside down onto a platter. It is popular throughout the Middle East, each region having its own variations. The Iraqi version stands out with its beautifully bright colours and warm, comforting layers.

Bring the water and salt to boil and add the rice. Boil for seven to ten minutes, drain, and set aside. Sauté the diced onions in oil until translucent. Add the salt, garlic, and tomato paste to coat the onions. Sauté for three to five minutes before adding the vegetable broth and diced tomato. Simmer for five minutes, add to the rice along with the lemon juice, and cook over a low heat.

Combine the date syrup, olive oil, and salt to coat the aubergine rounds and the onion slices. In batches, lightly pan fry the aubergine; cool on paper towels. Caramelize the onions, sauté the peppers with salt, and lightly pan fry the tomatoes; set aside each vegetable as they are ready.

Cover the bottom of a non-stick pot in oil. Layer the aubergine to cover the bottom; add the tomatoes, then the peppers, and the onions in layers. Finally, add the rice, flatten it down, and cook on a low heat for at least fifteen minutes.

To flip the maqluba, place a serving platter that is larger in diameter than the pot and quickly turn over. Top with parsley and serve with thick yoghurt.

Sara Leana Ahmad is an
Iraqi-American food blogger
at Add a Little Lemon.

Shatha Alimara Najib

Sweet red rice with date syrup

350g / 1½ cup
  long-grain rice
4 tbsp date syrup
5 cardamom pods
3 cinnamon sticks
1½ tbsp butter
½ tbsp sugar
½ tbsp salt
½ tsp saffron
½ tbsp ground
  cardamom
1.4–1.6l / 6–7 cups
  hot water

Serves 3–4

Fish, rice, and dates are all heavily consumed in Iraq, so it is only natural that this dish would be a national favourite. I like it with *masgouf*, a smoky, grilled Iraqi fish (see pages 106–9), or with *zubeidi*, fried butterfish. The sweetness of the rice complements and contrasts with the saltiness and spices of the fish.

In a bowl, rinse the rice with cold water several times until the water is clear, and soak the rinsed rice in water for one hour.

Add the saffron to 60ml / ¼ cup of hot water, stir in the sugar, and mix for more flavour and colour. In a medium-sized pot, pour the remaining hot water, salt, cinnamon, whole cardamom pods, and two tablespoons of date syrup, before bringing the pot to boil for three to four minutes. Add the soaked rice to the pot and keep boiling until the grain is soft and ready. Empty the pot into a colander and drain the rice.

In the used pot, now empty, add the saffron, sugar, and butter. Wait for the butter to melt and then add two tablespoons of date syrup, rice from the colander, and the ground cardamom. Flip your stirring spoon around and use the stick end to mix the rice gently without breaking the grain. Lower the heat and simmer the rice for fifteen to twenty minutes. Serve hot.

Shatha Alimara Najib is a London-based Iraqi cook and YouTuber.

Anissa Helou

Muhammar
Sweet-savoury rice

180ml / ⅔ cup date syrup
375ml / 1½ cups boiling
  water
4 cardamom pods, smashed
1 cinnamon stick
500g / 2½ cups basmati
  rice, soaked for 30 minutes
  in 2 litres (2 quarts) water
  and 1 tbsp salt
Sea salt
3 tbsp vegetable oil
1 tbsp ground cardamom
1 good pinch of saffron
  strands, steeped in
  60ml / ¼ cup of rose water

Serves 4–6

There are two ways of making this sweet-savoury rice. One is to caramelize sugar before adding water and parboiling the rice in the sweet water, then finishing the rice by steaming with a little butter or ghee and saffron rose water. The other method – my favourite – is to sweeten the rice with date syrup, which is what was done traditionally.

Put the date syrup in a large pot in which you will be cooking the rice. Add the boiling water, cardamom pods, and cinnamon stick and place over a medium heat. Bring to a boil, then drain the soaked rice and add to the pot. Stir the rice, bring back to a boil, and then reduce the heat to low and cover the pot. Let simmer for eight to ten minutes or until the liquid is fully absorbed. Check and taste for salt; add more if necessary.

Meanwhile, heat the oil in a small pan over a medium heat. When the rice is done, drizzle the hot oil over the rice and sprinkle the ground cardamom and saffron rose water all over. Use a fork to mix the rice and fluff it up. Wrap the lid with a clean kitchen towel and let the rice steam over a very low heat for ten more minutes. Fluff it up again with a fork and serve hot. It is an ideal accompaniment for the Arabian fried fish on pages 100–1.

Anissa Helou is a Syrian-Lebanese chef, broadcaster, and author of ten cookbooks.

Linda Dangoor

Timman w' basal
Onion rice

500g / 2½ cups basmati rice
650ml / 2¾ cups water
½ tsp vegetable stock or
  bouillon powder
1 large onion, halved
  and thinly sliced
1 big handful of raisins
3 tbsp olive oil
1 level tsp turmeric
Salt and pepper to taste

Serves 5–6

The sweetness of the onions and raisins makes this dish a good accompaniment to sweet stews or sweet-and-sour dishes that contain date syrup or tamarind molasses.

Wash the rice and soak for thirty minutes and then drain.

Heat the olive oil in a non-stick pot and gently fry the onions until they become dark brown and caramelized (but not burnt).

Add the water, the raisins, and vegetable stock and stir. The water will become brown.

Now add the drained rice to the water, stir gently, and bring to the boil. Continue boiling half-covered on a medium heat for about three minutes. Then reduce the heat to the lowest setting, cover, and cook for thirty minutes. Uncover, gently fluff up the rice, and sprinkle with a little olive oil. Cover and cook for another ten minutes.

You can either serve the rice straight away or continue to cook on the lowest setting for a further fifteen to twenty minutes to ensure the formation of a toasted crust at the bottom.

To serve as a cake, put a large plate on top of the pot, hold it firmly down with one hand, and turn the pot over with the other.

Linda Dangoor is an Iraqi artist
and food writer based in London.

Nawal Nasrallah

Yellow rice

3 tbsp oil
½ tsp turmeric
450g / 2 cups rice
    (if an aged variety is used,
    such as basmati, it needs
    to be washed and soaked
    for at least 30 minutes,
    and then drained)
825ml / 3½ cups water
1½ tsp salt
½ tsp ground cardamom
1 piece of cinnamon,
    2.5cm / 1in long

Serves 4

This easy-to-cook recipe for rice goes perfectly with the sweet-and-sour fish with raisin and date syrup sauce on pages 102–3.

In a medium-heavy pot (preferably non-stick), put all the rice ingredients and let them boil, covered, for seven to ten minutes on a high heat, until all visible moisture evaporates. Reduce heat to low and let it simmer for about fifteen minutes. Fold rice gently two to three times while simmering to allow it to fluff.

Nawal Nasrallah is an Iraqi scholar, food blogger, and cookbook author based in Boston, Massachusetts.

Reem Kassis

Teta Asma's tabbouleh

250g / 1½ cups coarse
  bulgur wheat
75g / 1½ cups flat-leaf
  parsley, finely chopped
25g / ½ cup mint,
  finely chopped
500g / 1lb 2oz medium
  tomatoes, finely diced
50g / ⅓ cup shelled
  pistachios, toasted
40g / ⅓ cup walnuts,
  chopped and toasted
50g / ⅓ cup raisins or sultanas
4 spring onions (scallions),
  finely chopped
50g / 1 cup pomegranate
  seeds (optional)

For the dressing
4 tbsp extra virgin olive oil
4 tbsp lemon juice
1½ tbsp pomegranate
  molasses (no added sugar)
1½ tbsp date syrup
1 tsp salt
½ tsp chilli flakes (optional)
¼ tsp ground black pepper
¼ tsp ground cumin
½ tsp dried marjoram, rubbed
  to a powder (optional)

Serves 4 as a main
  or 8 as a starter

Reem Kassis is a Palestinian
writer and cookbook author
based in Philadelphia.

The name of this dish is a little misleading, as it is not really tabbouleh salad at all. Its origins are as the stuffing that my grandmother Teta Asma would use for her vegetarian vine leaves. She preferred it to traditional tabbouleh – which is mostly parsley with a bit of fine bulgur – and I couldn't agree more.

Put the bulgur wheat into a salad bowl and cover with 350ml / 1½ cups of very hot or just boiled water. Stir, then set aside until the bulgur has absorbed the liquid and cooled, about thirty minutes.

Meanwhile, prepare all the remaining ingredients and make the dressing by putting all the ingredients into a small bowl and whisking until combined.

To assemble the salad, fluff up the bulgur wheat with a fork until the grains are separated. Add the chopped parsley and mint and toss to combine. Add the tomatoes and give them another gentle toss. Pour the dressing over the salad, then add the nuts and raisins and give one final toss to combine. Scatter with pomegranate seeds, if using.

The dish can be served immediately, but is best after one or two hours when the bulgur has had a chance to soak up all the flavours.

Fish

Soli Zardosht

Roasted sea bass with citrus and herbs

1 whole sea bass,
  scaled and gutted
Fine salt and freshly
  ground black pepper
1 lemon, sliced into
  thin rounds
½ orange, sliced into
  thin rounds
3 tbsp butter, divided
1 bunch of spring onions
  (scallions), thinly sliced
3 garlic cloves, sliced
10g / ¼ cup chopped
  coriander (cilantro)
1 tbsp chopped tarragon
½ tsp ground dried mint
2 tbsp pomegranate
  molasses
1½ tbsp date syrup
2 tbsp lemon juice
2 tbsp orange juice
1 tbsp orange zest
1 tsp saffron with
  2 tbsp warm water
1 tsp turmeric
1 tsp chilli powder
2 tbsp olive oil

Serves 2

I came up with this recipe while planning a *nowrooz* dinner (Persian new year), celebrated on the first day of spring in March. The use of date syrup balances the acidity of the citrus and pomegranate, and aids in the caramelization of the baked fish.

Preheat the oven to 220°C / 425°F / gas mark 7.

Rinse the fish, pat dry, make three slits on one side, and sprinkle salt over the outside and inside the cavity. Place on a lightly oiled tray lined with parchment paper, along with the sliced orange and most of the lemon (hold back a few slices).

Melt two tablespoons of the butter in a small frying pan over a medium heat. Add the spring onions and garlic, sautéing for about five minutes. Stir in the coriander (cilantro), tarragon, and mint, cooking for fifteen seconds until fragrant and wilted.

Stir in the pomegranate molasses, date syrup, orange and lemon juices, zest, saffron water, turmeric, pinch of salt, and chilli powder. Turn the heat to medium low, cooking for five minutes.

Rub the outside of the fish with olive oil, season with black pepper, and pack the herb mixture into the cavity. Fill the slashes with a little herb mixture, dot the cavity and cut sides with the remaining butter, and place the rest of the lemon inside the fish.

Roast until the flesh is opaque white and flaky, around twenty minutes. Grill for two minutes to crisp the outside. Serve immediately.

Soli Zardosht is an Iranian-British chef, running Zardosht with sister Sanaz across residencies in London and New York.

Anissa Helou

Samak meqli
Arabian spiced fried fish

4 whole sea bream, approx.
   300g / 10½oz each,
   or 2 Thai snappers,
   550g / 1lb 3oz each, scaled
   and gutted, fins removed
   (but not the heads or tails)
Sea salt
Plain flour, for dredging
Ground black pepper
B'zar (Arabian spice mixture)
Vegetable oil

For the marinade
3 garlic cloves, minced
1cm / ½in fresh ginger,
   minced
1 tbsp b'zar
   (Arabian spice mixture)
¼ tsp ground turmeric
¼ tsp ground black pepper
1 pinch of sea salt
Juice of ½ lemon

To serve
Lime or lemon wedges

Serves 4

This is a typical recipe from the Arabian Gulf, where many people cannot conceive of lunch without fish on the table. Often, restaurants will have both fish and meat for diners to choose from. This fried fish is particularly good served with sweet-savoury rice on pages 88–9, as the fish's spicy marinade provides a delectable contrast to the sweetish rice.

Mix the garlic, ginger, b'zar, turmeric, black pepper, sea salt, and lemon juice in a small bowl for the marinade.

Pat the fish dry with paper towels, then make two or three diagonal slashes across the flesh on both sides. Rub with a little salt inside and out and let it sit for five minutes.

Rub the marinade evenly over the fish, inside and out. Put in a dish and let the fish absorb the flavours for at least thirty minutes.

Put a little flour on a plate and season it with salt, pepper, and b'zar.

Set a wire rack in a rimmed baking sheet. Pour enough oil into a large skillet to cover the bottom and heat over a medium-high heat until hot. Working in batches, dip each fish into the seasoned flour on both sides, shaking off the excess, then slide in as many fish as will comfortably fit in the pan and fry for two to three minutes on each side. Remove with a slotted spoon and place on the wire rack to drain off any excess oil. Serve while still hot.

Anissa Helou is a Syrian-
Lebanese chef, broadcaster,
and author of ten cookbooks.

Nawal Nasrallah

Sweet-and-sour fish with raisin and date syrup sauce

900g / 2lb salmon,
 skinless boneless fillet,
 cut into 6 strips
1 tbsp oil
1 tbsp date syrup
1 tbsp yellow mustard
¼ tsp salt

For the sauce
1 medium onion, chopped,
 about 145g / 1 cup
2 tbsp oil
2 garlic cloves, thinly sliced
115g / ¾ cup raisins
60g / ½ cup walnuts,
 broken into pieces
30g / ¾ cup parsley,
 finely chopped
1½ tsp curry powder
1 tsp coriander seeds
 crushed
¾ tsp salt
¼ tsp black pepper
2 tbsp date syrup
1 tbsp lemon juice
60ml / ¾ cup water

Serves 6

Prepare a feast – truly delicious, satisfying, and healthy – in just half an hour. I use salmon for this recipe, but feel free to substitute for your favourite variety of fish.

In a medium skillet and on a medium heat, sauté onion in oil until translucent. Add the garlic, raisins, walnuts, and parsley, stirring frequently until fragrant. Add the curry powder, coriander, salt, and black pepper, and stir well for about thirty seconds. Add the date syrup, lemon juice, and water, and let them simmer on a low heat, uncovered, stirring until the sauce thickens; keep warm.

Turn on the grill (broiler). Line a shallow baking pan with foil and drizzle with half a tablespoon of oil. Arrange the fish pieces on the pan, leaving space between them. Mix the date syrup and mustard in a small bowl, and brush the fish with it, coating the pieces lightly. Drizzle with the remaining oil and a light sprinkle of salt.

Grill (broil) the fish for five minutes, then turn the pieces over and brush with the mustard and syrup mix. Sprinkle with salt and cook until surface is crisp and golden.

Spread yellow rice (see pages 92–3) on a platter, arrange the fish on top, and spread the raisin and date syrup sauce between and around the fish pieces. Serve immediately.

Nawal Nasrallah is an Iraqi scholar, food blogger, and cookbook author based in Boston, Massachusetts.

Nuno Mendes

Oven-baked salmon with date syrup

1 large side of sustainably
  farmed salmon, filleted,
  trimmed, scales removed
  and pin-boned
  (approx. 2.7kg / 6lb)
450g / 1⅓ cup date
  syrup, plus enough to
  glaze after cooking
200g / ⅘ cup Maldon salt
Zest of 1 unwaxed orange
Sprigs of bronze fennel, dill,
  or fennel flowers to garnish

Serves 4–6

It is so poignant to see such a beautiful product coming out of a torn country. The product has infinite possibilities. I was particularly excited to work with it on a savoury recipe. The sweetness and natural nuttiness works really well with the fattiness of the salmon. I have realized now that date syrup is not particularly easy to find, but it is a product I would love to have both in my pantry at home and in the stock cupboard of my working kitchens.

Pat the salmon dry and rub with salt on all sides before doing the same with the date syrup. The mix should be pastelike: apply it over and under the fish.

Place the fish on a tray, skin side down, and cover with a lid or cling film. Cure in the salt and syrup for four hours. You can keep it at room temperature to speed up the curing process – if you refrigerate the fish, it will take longer to cure. Once cured, drain the liquid and wash in cold water to remove the salt, pat dry, and glaze again with more date syrup.

Cook at 60 °C / 140 °F / gas mark 1 for thirty minutes on a rack placed in a deep tray, with the fish skin side down. The tray underneath will capture the juices from the salmon and can be used to glaze, along with more date syrup. Glaze again thoroughly using a brush, and transfer the fish to a serving platter.

Garnish with the orange zest, sprigs of bronze fennel, dill, or fennel flowers if you can find them.

Nuno Mendes, originally from Portugal, is the executive chef at Chiltern Firehouse and Mãos in London.

Michael Rakowitz

Masgouf
Barbecued fish with date syrup marinade

2 freshwater carp, each
approx. 450g / 16oz

For the basting sauce
215g / 1 cup sesame or
olive oil
240ml / 1 cup warm water
2 tbsp Iraqi date syrup
1 tbsp cumin
1 tbsp curry
1 tbsp sea salt
1 tsp tamarind

Serves 2

Masgouf is considered the national dish of Iraq. Dating back to ancient Babylon, the basic recipe consists of a fresh carp fished from the Tigris River, split open from the back, gutted, and impaled on two wooden stakes next to an open fire of apricot logs, fig logs, or reeds. In 2007, Baghdad's imams issued a fatwa on the carp swimming in the Tigris and Euphrates rivers, declaring them unclean and unfit for human consumption due to the large number of corpses floating in the waterways. And so, at the height of the war, another of Iraq's cultural symbols was endangered.

To make the basting sauce, mix the ingredients thoroughly and place in a squeezable condiment bottle.

You can cook the fish over a barbecue using a grill basket, but to prepare *masgouf* the traditional way, a firepit is required.

First, catch a carp. This is hard to do. Fishermen call them the 'golden ghost' for a reason.

Kill the carp. A swift whack to the head using a wooden club is the least painful way to achieve this.

Using a sharp gutting knife, cut the fish open from the back – not the belly – starting below the dorsal fin and slicing towards the tail. Then slice down the middle of the head. If the head is hard, use scissors to do this.

Open the fish so that it is butterflied. Remove the stomach and innards carefully. Be careful not to puncture the gall bladder as this will give your fish a metallic taste if it bleeds.

Do not scale the fish. Near the spine, to the right and left of the dorsal fin, make two incisions on the back using the knife.

Firmly plant two skewers or sharpened sticks into the ground. They should have a distance between them to

correspond to the incisions made in the fish. Their length depends on the size of the fish, but there should be at least twenty-five centimetres / ten inches between the ground and the fish.

Insert the two skewers or sticks into the incisions.

With the carp now butterflied open and standing vertically, build a fire using natural, dried wood beside the open belly of the fish. Be careful not to use construction timber, as pressure-treated wood will release toxic gases.

Light the fire and allow the fish to slowly cook and smoke. Depending on the size of your fish, this process could take between forty-five minutes and three hours. Throughout the cooking, baste your fish with the sauce by spraying or brushing it on the meat. You will know your fish is cooked when the eyes become foggy or completely white.

Carefully remove the fish from the skewers or sticks. The fish becomes more delicate and flaky when it cooks, so be sure to cradle it with both hands.

Rake the burning embers of the fire to evenly distribute them like coals across the pit.

Lay the fish on foil, skin face down, and place onto the embers. Allow the fish to cook through a bit more, until you see liquid beginning to boil on its surface. You may also baste the fish one last time.

Remove the fish. Place on a round tray and garnish with lettuce and lemons. Serve with *tannour* bread and *amba* (pickled mango). Eat with your hands and share.

Michael Rakowitz is an Iraqi-American artist and professor based in Chicago.

Sam and Sam Clark

Deep-fried fish heads with date syrup sauce

1–2 large hake heads
Salt
2–3 tbsp plain flour
500–700ml / 2–3 cups
  sunflower or rapeseed oil
  for deep frying
Rocket and lemon
  wedges to serve

For the sauce
4 tbsp date syrup
3 tbsp sherry vinegar
½ tsp ground coriander
2 tbsp extra virgin olive oil
½ garlic clove, crushed
  with a little salt
¾ tsp green chilli, deseeded
  and finely chopped
1 tbsp coriander
  (cilantro), chopped
1 pinch of brown sugar
  (optional)

Serves 2–4

Fish are precious and rare, so when we receive a large hake, sea bass, or turbot from the coast, we never throw the head away. We have learnt over the years that it is a thing to be prized. Mostly the cheeks are the real delicacy, yet there are surprisingly delicious pickings to be had all over. Ask your fishmonger to put some heads aside for you. We deep fry them because it is quick and you achieve a little bit of crunch on the skin. The alternative is to omit the flour and bake the heads, covered with foil.

Season the heads all over with salt, rubbing it in slightly. Allow the salt to penetrate for at least ten minutes. Place the vinegar, date syrup, ground coriander, and olive oil in a small saucepan and simmer over a medium heat for three minutes, until reduced. Add a splash or two of water to give a light, smooth, saucy consistency. Add the garlic, green chilli, and chopped coriander (cilantro). Taste and season with salt, brown sugar, and a pinch of black pepper, then pour into a small serving bowl or ramekin.

Coat the fish heads thickly with the flour. In a saucepan large enough to fry one head at a time, heat up sufficient oil to cover it over a medium-high heat. Carefully lower each fish head into the oil one at a time and fry until it is a dark golden colour. Remove and place on a paper towel to drain. We recommend eating this dish with your fingers and spooning on bits of the sauce as you go.

Sam and Sam Clark are British restaurateurs, founders of Moro and Morito in London.

Meat and Poultry

Nasrin Rooghani

Lamb Baharat

1 joint of lamb, trimmed
2 or 3 large carrots,
  peeled, trimmed, and
  cut into large pieces
1 large onion, peeled and
  cut into thick wedges
Sea salt

For the Baharat spice mix
2 tsp cumin seeds
1 tsp each coriander seeds,
  black peppercorns, allspice
½ tsp cloves
20 green cardamom pods
1 small cinnamon stick
⅓ whole nutmeg (or grate
  equivalent amount)

Serves 6

I am so glad to have been introduced to cooking with date syrup. It is not just sweet; it has different levels and a depth to it that I cannot completely describe. For this dish, the meat is best seasoned with sea salt the day before: season, wrap, and chill. This quantity of spice mix is enough for one lamb joint.

To make the spice mix, toast the cumin and coriander seeds gently for a minute or two in a dry frying pan until they start releasing aroma. Do not allow them to burn. Put all the ingredients together into a spice grinder or a mortar and pestle, and grind to a fine powder. If you do not have this equipment, use equivalent quantities of ground spices instead.

Bring the lamb to room temperature before cooking. Season with a layer of sea salt rubbed into the meat. In a hot skillet or frying pan, heat a little oil and sear the meat on all sides. Remove from the heat and rest until cool enough to handle.

Add olive oil and date syrup to the spice mix – about one tablespoon of each – to turn the powder into a paste. Put the lamb into a roasting tin, cover with the spice paste using your hands, and add carrots and onion. Add about 500ml / 2 cups of water to the dish: this will turn into stock as the lamb cooks.

Take sheets of greaseproof paper and cooking foil, tucking over and around the meat (paper inside, foil outside). Seal tightly. Bake at 180°C / 350°F / gas mark 4 for at least two hours. The lamb should be browned on the outside, sitting in a shallow layer of stock, and tender enough to pull easily away from the bone when it is done. Serve on plain steamed rice and cooked lentils, using or discarding the vegetables as you please. Garlic *torshi* (see pages 222–3) would be a great accompaniment.

Nasrin Rooghani is an Iranian
chef with the social enterprise
Mazi Mas in London.

Claudia Roden

Roast shoulder of lamb with couscous and date stuffing

1 shoulder of lamb
Salt and black pepper
250g / 1½ cups
  medium-grain couscous
1 tbsp orange blossom water
1 tsp ground cinnamon
2 tbsp sunflower or
  vegetable oil
150g / 1 cup dates, stoned
  and cut into small pieces
50g / ⅓ cup seedless raisins
100g / ⅔ cup blanched
  almonds, chopped coarsely
65g / ⅓ cup butter,
  cut into small pieces
2 tbsp date syrup, plus more
  to pass around in the jar
To garnish: 8–12 dates and
  8 blanched almonds

Serves 6

Dates have something of a sacred character in an Arab desert culture. A favourite food of the Prophet Mohammad is said to have been hays, a mixture of dates, butter, and milk. He also liked fat meat. When a lamb or a kid was being cooked, he would go to the pot, take out the shoulder, and eat it.

Put the joint skin side up in a baking dish or roasting pan, sprinkle with salt and pepper, and roast in an oven preheated to 250°C / 400°F / gas mark 6 for twenty minutes. Then lower the heat to 160°C / 320°F / gas mark 3 and cook for four to five hours until the skin is crisp and brown and the meat is juicy and meltingly tender. Pour off the fat after about two hours.

Put the couscous in another baking dish, adding the same volume of warm water – about 300ml / 1¼ cups, with a little salt, orange blossom water, and cinnamon, and stir well. After ten minutes, add the oil and rub the grain between your fingers to air. Mix in the remaining ingredients, apart from the butter, cover with foil, and put in the oven with the lamb for the last twenty minutes.

Cover the meat with two tablespoons of date syrup. Stir the butter into the couscous and fluff with a fork, seasoning to taste.

Remove the stones from the dates and replace with blanched almonds. Serve the meat with the couscous stuffing decorated with these dates.

Claudia Roden is an Egyptian-
British cookbook writer and
cultural anthropologist.

Thomasina Miers

Falling-apart lamb shoulder with date syrup, chickpeas, fennel, and chilli

1 lamb shoulder, approx.
  2kg / 4½lb, bone in and
  trimmed of excess fat
4 sprigs of thyme
1 tsp dried oregano
5 garlic cloves
2 tsp each cumin
  and fennel seeds
1 tbsp coriander seeds
1 tsp each ground paprika
  and cinnamon
4 tbsp extra virgin olive oil
4 tbsp date syrup
2 red onions,
  roughly chopped

For the chickpeas
250g / 1¼ cups dried
  chickpeas, soaked overnight
1 small bunch of parsley
1 tsp peppercorns

To serve
A couscous salad flecked
  with masses of coriander
  and parsley

Serves 6–8

The rich depths of the date syrup give this slow-cooked lamb a wonderfully complex sweetness and the resulting caramelization is quite irresistible!

Preheat the oven to 190°C / 375°F / gas mark 5. Take the lamb out of the fridge and leave to come to room temperature. With a mortar and pestle, bash the thyme together with the oregano, two garlic cloves, and a teaspoon of salt to make a rough paste. Warm the cumin, fennel, and coriander seeds in a dry frying pan over a medium heat and, when fragrant, add to the mortar with the paprika and cinnamon, and grind to a paste. Add the olive oil and date syrup and mix thoroughly. Make shallow slashes all over the lamb, then rub in two-thirds of the paste and season well with salt and pepper. Toss the onions in the rest of the paste and place in a deep roasting tin with the lamb on top and 100ml / ½ cup water in the bottom of the pan. Cover with foil, put in the oven, and roast for half an hour. After that time, turn the heat down to 160°C / 320°F / gas mark 3 and roast for another ninety minutes.

While the lamb is cooking, drain the soaked chickpeas and put in a large pan covered by between seven and eight centimetres / three inches of cold water. Smash the remaining three cloves of garlic, add the parsley and peppercorns, and simmer for one to two hours until the chickpeas are tender, seasoning them with a teaspoon of salt when they start softening. Remove the foil from the lamb, add the chickpeas, and cook for another hour or so until the meat is tender enough to pull apart with two forks. Serve with lemon wedges and a couscous salad dotted with pomegranate seeds, roughly chopped parsley and coriander, and finely chopped red onion.

Thomasina Miers is an English cook, writer, television presenter, and co-founder of the Wahaca restaurant group.

Sarit Packer and Itamar Srulovich

Sofrito
Short ribs with dates, date syrup, and potatoes

3 tbsp vegetable oil
850g / 1lb 14oz beef
  short ribs
2 tsp sea salt
½ tsp freshly ground
  black pepper
2 onions, peeled
  (about 350g / 2 cups)
2 potatoes, peeled
  (about 450g / 2 cups)
1 tbsp tomato purée
60g / ⅓ cup dried
  pitted dates
120ml / ½ cup water
2 tbsp date syrup, to glaze

Serves 2, with leftovers

Sofrito is the signature dish of Jerusalem. The name comes from the Ladino dialect, a kind of pidgin Spanish spoken by the oldest Jewish community there. Sofrito is the essence of the simple, no-frills, salt-and-pepper cooking typical of this town. The scent of it is the essential smell of home.

Heat the oil in a large frying pan on a high heat. Place the short ribs flat side down in the pan and season with the salt and pepper. Brown one side at a time (about three to four minutes on each). Cut each onion into six wedges and each potato into eight wedges.

Remove the ribs from the pan and place in a large ovenproof pot, leaving the pan on the heat. Put the onions in the pan and colour a little (two to three minutes). Add the potato wedges, cooking for a further two minutes. Add the tomato purée, stir to coat the vegetables, then tip the contents of the pan onto the meat in the ovenproof pot.

Add the dates and water, cover the pot and cook – either simmer it on a very low heat or place it in the oven at 160°C / 320°F / gas mark 3 (or 140°C / 275°F in a fan oven) for three to four hours, or, even better, cook at 150°C / 300°F / gas mark 2 (130°C / 250°F fan oven) overnight. Before serving, brush the meat with the date syrup to make it shiny and sweet.

Chefs Sarit Packer and Itamar
Srulovich run London's Honey & Co.,
Honey & Smoke, and Honey & Spice.

Reem Kassis

Kofta hamees

800g / 1¾lb coarsely
   ground meat (beef, lamb,
   veal, or a combination)
100g / 3½oz pitta (pita)
   bread or white bread with
   crust removed, roughly torn
1 tomato, quartered
1 small onion,
   coarsely chopped
2 garlic cloves
1 green chilli (optional)
2 tbsp chopped coriander
2 tbsp chopped flat-leaf
   parsley
1 tbsp tomato paste
1 tbsp olive oil
1 tbsp salt
1 tbsp nine spice mix,
   or substitute with Lebanese
   seven spice or Baharat
   spice mix (see page 117)

Makes 25–30 meatballs

This dish is a contrast of sweet and sour: sweet from the date syrup, sour from the pomegranate molasses and tomato paste. The toasted pine nuts also give a desirable crunch to the tender meatballs, which pair perfectly with white or vermicelli rice and a side of cucumber yoghurt.

Preheat the oven to 220 °C / 425 °F / gas mark 7. Place about one quarter of the meat in a large mixing bowl and set aside.

In a food processor, combine the bread, tomato, onion, garlic, chilli, coriander, parsley, olive oil, salt, and spice mix. Pulse to a coarse paste, pour over the meat in the bowl, and mix with your hands until fully combined. Add in the remaining meat and mix gently, just until evenly distributed. Shape the mixture into golfball-sized balls. Place in a single layer on a baking sheet, and oven-cook until they start to brown, fifteen to twenty minutes. Remove from oven and set aside.

For the sauce, heat olive oil in a heavy-bottomed saucepan until shimmering but not smoking. Add in the sliced onions and cook on a medium-high heat until golden brown, ten to fifteen minutes. Add in tomato paste and stir for another minute.

Pour a little chicken stock over the onions, add date syrup and pomegranate molasses, season with salt and pepper, and bring to a boil. Reduce heat and simmer for ten minutes. Taste and season to your liking.

Reem Kassis is a Palestinian
writer and cookbook author
based in Philadelphia.

Cameron Emirali

Chicken, sage, and date polpetti

500g / 1lb 2oz skinless
  chicken thighs
50g / 1¼ cups fresh sage
50g / ⅓ cup fresh Medjool
  dates, diced
1 pinch of dried chilli
Zest of 1 lemon
50ml / 3½ tbsp date syrup
2 egg whites
Salt and pepper

For the lemon polenta
500ml / 2⅛ cups water
500ml / 2⅛ cups milk
200g / 1¼ cups polenta
Sage stalks
2 garlic cloves
2 lemons, zested and
  squeezed
1 pinch of dried chilli
Olive oil
50g / ¼ cup parmesan

Serves 4–5

I was working as head chef at The Wapping Project in east London when I first developed this recipe. It was originally intended as a stuffing for whole quail, but I think it works just as well made into individual polpetti. I particularly like how well the earthiness of the sage balances the sweetness of the dates in the dish.

Blitz the chicken and two egg whites in a food processor, and put the mix into a bowl. Add the diced dates, lemon zest, chilli, sage, date syrup, salt, and pepper before rolling the mixture into balls. Line a baking tray with parchment paper, arrange the meatballs on the tray, and then bake them in the oven at 180°C / 350°F / gas mark 4 for twelve minutes.

To make your polenta, boil the milk with sage stalks, garlic, chilli, lemon juice, zest, and olive oil. Once boiled, put the mixture to one side to infuse for twenty minutes and strain. After straining, bring it back to boil, whisk in the polenta and simmer while stirring for twenty minutes. When the mixture has thickened and found the right consistency, grate in the parmesan and drizzle with olive oil. Season with salt and pepper to taste.

To serve, sit the meatballs on the polenta and finish with fried sage and more grated parmesan.

Cameron Emirali is a New Zealand restaurateur and co-owner of 10 Greek Street in London.

Asma Khan

Tangra chicken kebab skewers

500g / 1lb 2oz skinless
and boneless chicken thighs
2 garlic cloves
3cm / 1½in fresh ginger
6 tbsp light or superior
soy sauce
1½ tbsp lime juice
1 tsp ground coriander
1 tbsp date syrup
(and a bit extra to
brush the kebab)
1 tsp cayenne pepper
½ tsp toasted sesame seeds

Serves 4

Chinese of Haka origin have been settling in Bengal since the eighteenth century. India's only Chinatown is in Calcutta: Tangra. The Chinese eateries in Tangra use a distinct kind of locally produced soy sauce called 'red sauce'. While it is not actually red, it is a little sweet. Here, I have added date syrup for that 'red sauce' taste in the soy-sauce marinade.

Cut the chicken into cubes, around two centimetres / one inch each. Crush the ginger and garlic with a mortar and pestle or a food processor and add the soy sauce, lime juice, date syrup, ground coriander, and cayenne pepper to make a marinade. Mix the marinade with the chicken, making sure all the pieces are covered. Leave the meat to marinate – ideally overnight, but for a minimum of two hours. Always bring the chicken to room temperature before cooking.

These kebabs can be cooked on an outdoor barbecue or an indoor grill (broiler). Use metal skewers for a barbecue (this quantity should require four) or bamboo skewers for indoor cooking. If you are inside, make sure not to burn the exposed bamboo, and use as many as necessary (around eight centimetres / three inches of chicken per bamboo skewer) to ensure all the meat is under the heat, ideally ten to twelve centimetres / four to five inches away. The chicken should take four to five minutes to cook on each side. Once cooked and browned, remove from heat, brush with date syrup, and sprinkle toasted sesame seeds on the kebabs before serving.

Asma Khan is an Indian writer, entrepreneur, and founder of Darjeeling Express in London.

Michael Rakowitz

Iraqi fried chicken

900g / 2lb chicken wings
 (or parts of your choice)
900g / 2lb chicken legs
 (or parts of your choice)
375g / 3 cups flour
6 eggs
1 tbsp salt
120g / 2 cups breadcrumbs
½ tbsp sumac
2–3 tbsp Iraqi Baharat spice
 mix (cumin, dried limes,
 turmeric, ginger, chilli,
 curry, cloves, cardamom,
 dried rose petals, allspice;
 or see page 117)
1 tbsp Iraqi date syrup
1 bottle olive or sesame oil

Serves 6–7

After eight sessions learning how to cook Iraqi food, my students at the Hudson Guild Community Center in New York proposed that they teach me something about their families' recipes in return. Hyasheem asked, 'Do Iraqis make Southern fried chicken?' I answered that no, to my knowledge, there was nothing like it in Iraqi cuisine. 'Well, then let's invent it', he said.

Break the eggs into a bowl and beat to an even consistency. In a plastic bag, mix the flour, salt, spices, date syrup, and breadcrumbs. Dip a piece of chicken in the egg and place it in the bag. Repeat until about six pieces of chicken are in the bag. Close the bag tightly and shake vigorously, so that the mixture of flour and spices covers each piece.

In a deep pan, pour enough oil so that it is about a half a centimetre / quarter of an inch deep. Place on stove and let heat for two minutes. Place the six pieces of chicken in the pan and fry, turning often, until each side is medium brown.

Repeat these steps until all the chicken is cooked.

Serve with a side of yellow rice (see pages 92–3), garlic *torshi* (see pages 222–3), and amba (pickled mango).

Michael Rakowitz is an Iraqi-American
artist and professor based in Chicago.

Eleanor Ford

Venetian almond milk chicken with saffron and dates

8 skin-on, bone-in
  chicken thighs
1 tbsp plain flour
3 tbsp olive oil
2 small onions,
  finely chopped
60g / ¼ cup ginger,
  peeled and finely chopped
4 garlic cloves, finely
  chopped
1 tsp ground cinnamon
½ tsp grated nutmeg
½ tsp ground coriander
1 pinch of ground cloves
2 bay leaves
400ml / 1⅓ cups
  unsweetened almond milk
2 tbsp verjuice (optional)
1 pinch of saffron
2 tbsp date syrup
4 dried dates, stoned and
  quartered
2 tbsp toasted almond
  flakes, to serve
1 handful of fresh coriander
  (cilantro), to serve

Serves 4

This recipe is based on one handwritten in a fourteenth-century cookbook from Venice. At the time, the city lay at the end of the fabled Silk Road, the European hub of spices and silks arriving from the East. Just as Venetian art and architecture drew on Islamic influence, so too can you see it in this sweetly spiced braise.

Season the chicken thighs generously with salt and pepper, and then dust with the flour.

Set a large casserole pan over a medium-high heat and, when hot, add the olive oil. Add the chicken thighs and brown to a deep gold on all sides. Remove to a plate, leaving the oil behind.

Add the onions to the pan and cook to soften but not colour. Stir in the ginger, garlic, spices, and bay leaves and cook for a couple of minutes longer until fragrant. Return the chicken thighs to the pan in a layer.

Pour in the almond milk and verjuice, scrunch in the strands of saffron, and add the syrup and whole dates. Season with salt. Bring to a bubble then lower the heat and simmer uncovered for one hour. The chicken should be tender and falling from the bone.

Remove the chicken with a slotted spoon and turn up the heat. Bubble the sauce until it has reduced and thickened. Taste for seasoning and adjust as needed. Serve in the sauce, scattered with toasted almonds and fresh coriander (cilantro).

Eleanor Ford is a British food writer and cookbook author specializing in Asian and world foods.

Shatha Alimara Najib

Halu w' hamid
Sweet-and-sour chicken

5–6 pieces (approx.
  600g / 1lb 5oz) chicken
  breast, cut into large strips
3 tbsp date syrup
3 tbsp olive oil
1 tbsp nigella seeds
Parsley (to garnish)

For the marinade
1 medium onion, grated
½ tsp salt
1 tsp black pepper
1 tsp chilli flakes
100ml / ½ cup soy sauce
3 tbsp olive oil
5–7 garlic cloves, mashed
  (approx. 20g / ¾oz)
5–7 ginger pieces, mashed
  (approx. 20g / ¾oz)
1 tsp sugar (brown or white)

Serves 2–3

A Middle Eastern take on the classic sweet-and-sour chicken, this glaze is fruity with slight heat and can be served with rice or vegetables. Don't worry about leftovers – if there are any, it is also great as a sandwich topping cold or hot the next day.

Mix the marinade ingredients together in a medium-sized bowl. Add the chicken pieces to the marinade, mix again, and place in the fridge for an hour or two – or overnight for more flavour.

Once the meat is ready, drizzle olive oil into a deep pan and immediately add the marinated chicken. Keep stirring until the sauce has almost evaporated and the chicken is blistered. Add the date syrup and stir for another minute. Be careful not to overcook, as the date syrup can become bitter.

Turn off the heat, and garnish with nigella seeds and parsley. The chicken is best eaten hot.

Shatha Alimara Najib is a London-based Iraqi cook and YouTuber.

Linda Dangoor

Silan chicken

4 chicken thighs
175g / ½ cup date syrup
2 tbsp balsamic vinegar
1 or 2 tbsp lemon juice
1 tsp lemon zest
60ml / ¼ cup olive oil
3 plump garlic cloves,
   crushed
¼ tsp cumin powder
1 pinch or more of cayenne
   or Aleppo pepper
1 tbsp salt or to taste

Serves 2

My family love the *silan* (date syrup) that comes from Basra
because it has the most authentic taste. It is a wonderful
addition to savoury dishes. I used it to make this delicious
chicken marinade.

Preheat the oven to 190°C / 375°F (fan) / gas mark 5.
   Mix all the marinade ingredients in a bowl.
   Place the chicken thighs in an oven dish and pour the
marinade over them. Mix very well using your hands. Leave to
marinate for at least thirty minutes.
   Cover and bake for fifteen minutes, then continue baking,
uncovered, for forty minutes or so, basting several times.
   Serve with rice or sweet potato mash.

Linda Dangoor is an Iraqi artist
and food writer based in London.

Yvonne Rakowitz

Silan marinade

2 chicken cutlets
2½ tbsp date syrup
½–1 tbsp (to taste)
  balsamic vinegar
3 tbsp lemon juice
1 medium onion or
  4 spring onions (scallions),
  chopped
1 handful of chopped
  nuts (pecans, walnuts,
  or almonds)
Chopped dates (optional)

To serve
200g / 1 cup basmati rice
  (on the side)

Serves 2

This *silan* (date syrup) recipe can be used for any meat, chicken, or even fish. These are basic measurements and serve as a ratio of the ingredients in the marinade. Just make sure that the meat is one-third submerged and you turn it over so that both sides have been marinated for at least one hour.

After marinating for at least an hour, remove the cutlets from the liquid (hold on to it!) and fry them, with just enough olive oil to coat the pan, until both sides are brown. Place in an oil-coated or non-stick pan and put in the oven at 180°C / 350°F / gas mark 4 for thirty minutes or until fully cooked. While the cutlets are cooking, boil the rice and drain.

In the same pan that you fried the cutlets, fry either chopped onions or spring onions (scallions) until transparent. Add the chopped nuts (pecans, walnuts, or almonds) to the pan and stir for another minute or two; you can also add chopped dates to the mixture. Add the rice and stir. Continue cooking for another few minutes, add the remaining marinade to the rice mixture, and continue to stir fry on a high-medium flame until the marinade is absorbed by the rice.

Serve the cutlets, garnishing with a drizzle of date syrup and chopped nuts, with the rice on the side.

Yvonne Rakowitz, the mother of
Iraqi-American artist Michael
Rakowitz, has worked with her son
to preserve and pass on her family's
Iraqi culture and traditional cooking.

Rosie Sykes

Spiced glazed duck

1 duck, approx. 2kg / 4½ lb
1 tsp sunflower oil
2 tsp salt
1 tsp ground cinnamon
½ tsp ground allspice
½ tsp ground ginger
½ tsp smoked chilli
  or pimenton
160g / ½ cup date syrup
2 tbsp dark soy sauce
2 tsp apple juice
2 tbsp sherry vinegar or
  lemon juice
2 tsp Dijon mustard

Serves 4–6

This is a delicious dish for a special occasion and very low maintenance to prepare.

It is best to take the duck out of the fridge and allow it to come to room temperature before cooking. Once the duck is out, pull out any large lumps of fat from inside and use a fork to make some perforations around the legs and the base of the breasts. Mix together all the spices with the salt, rubbing sunflower oil and then spice mix (very thoroughly!) all over the bird. Leave it to sit for an hour while preheating the oven to 150°C / 300°F / gas mark 3. Roast the duck for two hours.

For the glaze, mix the date syrup, soy sauce, apple juice, vinegar, and mustard in a bowl. When the duck has had its time, remove it from the oven, pour off any fat from the tin and baste generously with the glaze.

Turn the oven up to 190°C / 375°F / gas mark 5 (170°C / 340°F fan) and roast for a further twenty minutes until sticky and bronzed. Allow it to rest for at least twenty minutes before serving.

Serve with the cashew nut carrots on page 53 and steamed greens or simple rice noodles tossed with the juices from the duck pan.

Rosie Sykes is a British
chef and food writer.

Stephen Harris

Pheasant with bread sauce, cavolo nero, and date syrup

2 pheasant crowns
Goose fat
Salt and pepper

For the bread sauce
500ml / 2⅛ cup milk
1 medium onion,
  roughly chopped
6 cloves
A couple of twists of pepper
1 bay leaf
100g / 1⅓ cup slightly
  dried breadcrumbs
Nutmeg
80g / ⅓ cup butter

For the cavolo nero
1 head of cavolo nero
Salt
Date syrup to drizzle

Serves 4

Pheasant has a complex, creamy, slightly almondy taste, which makes chicken seem very bland in comparison. Avoid overcooking it and pheasant can be truly delicious. This recipe is adapted from an old favourite, where we use locally sourced rosehip syrup in place of the date syrup here.

Season the pheasant crowns with salt and pepper to taste. Brown the seasoned pheasant crowns in goose fat and roast in a low oven – 100°C / 210°F / gas mark 1 – for about thirty minutes until a probe reads 60°C / 140°F. Leave to rest for at least fifteen minutes. Remove the breasts and divide in two.

For the bread sauce, heat the milk and add the cloves, bay leaf, and onion and infuse overnight. Strain the milk and heat until it is simmering. Add the breadcrumbs and keep stirring until the sauce thickens. Add the pepper, salt, and nutmeg to taste.

To prepare the cabbage, slice the cavolo nero into thin strips and deep fry in oil at 180°C / 350°F. Drain on paper towel and season well with salt.

Just before serving, whisk the butter into the bread sauce. Do not leave it to melt as it must stay emulsified – rather like a risotto.

To serve, put a spoonful of bread sauce in the middle of a plate and rest the pheasant on top. Add the fried cabbage and drizzle the date syrup.

Stephen Harris is a British food writer and chef-patron of The Sportsman restaurant in Whitstable, Kent.

Sam and Sam Clark

Grilled quail with date syrup

4 quails, spatchcocked
  (see page 147)

Marinade
1 garlic clove, crushed
  to a paste with salt
½ medium onion, grated
2 level tsp ground cinnamon
1 level tsp ground cumin
2 tbsp date syrup
1 dsp olive oil

To serve
Extra date syrup
2 tbsp fresh mint, chopped
2 tbsp pistachios, chopped
2 tbsp pomegranate seeds

Serves 4

We never really cook anything the same twice – even the classics. For twenty years, we have changed the menu every three weeks. It is like cooking for the first time – very nerve-wracking, and very thrilling. You are only ever as good as your last meal, and you have to really expose yourself and put yourself on the line. It is like a new performance each time. This simple quail recipe, adapted from a previous favourite in the restaurant, is improved by using one's hands to devour it.

Mix all the marinade ingredients together and rub all over the quail. Place in a dish and marinate for at least two hours or in the fridge overnight.

To grill the quail, rub the tiniest amount of olive oil onto the bird and place breast side up on the barbecue (or hot griddle pan or domestic grill). Cook for five to eight minutes, depending on the heat, then turn over, and season with salt and pepper. Cook for another five minutes or until the meat is no longer pink but still juicy.

Transfer the quail to a plate and drizzle over more date syrup, followed by the mint, pistachios, and pomegranate seeds.

Sam and Sam Clark are British restaurateurs, founders of Moro and Morito in London.

Jason Hammel

Fried quail with smoked date syrup sauce and cashew butter

4 quails

For the marinade
50g / ¼ cup sugar
60g / ¼ cup salt
950ml / 4 cups water
1 cinnamon stick
2 pieces star anise
1 tsp cumin
2l / ½ gallon buttermilk

For the dredge
95g / ⅔ cup rice flour
15g / 1½ tbsp cornflour
30g / 2¾ tbsp potato flour

For the sauce
235g / ⅔ cup date syrup
80ml / ⅓ cup water
1 dried arbol chilli
6 dried dates

For the cashew butter
150g / 1 cup cashews
85g / ⅜ cup butter
30g / 1¾ tbsp red miso
1 lemon, zested
2 tsp lemon juice
⅛ tsp cayenne pepper
85g water

Serves 4

The sweet, dark date syrup and lively biting chilli banter with each other like friends in a good-natured, passionate squabble. They heighten each other's best qualities. Without the chilli, the syrup is too sweet, too simple. Without the syrup, the arbol would be too aggressive. But together everything comes alive.

For the marinade, combine all its ingredients except the buttermilk in a saucepan and bring to a simmer. Remove from the heat and allow the brine to cool completely. Pour over the quails and leave in the fridge overnight. After twelve hours, remove the quails from the brine and soak in the buttermilk.

For the dredge, combine all its ingredients in a shallow pan. Meanwhile, to prepare the cashew butter, use a food processor to blend the cashews and water until a loose paste forms. Add miso, spices, and lemon and slowly incorporate cubes of butter. Spin until the mixture is smooth, and then pass through a fine mesh strainer.

For the date syrup sauce, smoke dates over hardwood until fragrant. Allow to cool, slice thin, and combine with all the sauce's ingredients in a small saucepan. Reduce the mixture by a third, infusing the smoke and chilli flavour.

In a large Dutch oven or heavy pot, heat one litre / four cups of neutral cooking oil to 180°C / 350°F. Remove the quails from the buttermilk and toss in the dredge until they are coated. Now add the quails, two at a time, to the hot oil and fry until crispy and gold – it will take about five minutes. Remove the first two quails from the oil and set on a rimmed baking sheet with a wire rack while you fry the second pair.

In a mixing bowl, gently toss the fried quails in 115g / ½ cup of cashew butter and drizzle with smoked date syrup. Serve with sliced lemon and a dash of sumac.

Jason Hammel is an American restaurateur and the chef behind Chicago's Marisol and Lula Café.

Margot Henderson

Marinated and grilled quail

6 quails, spatchcocked
  (see method)
4 garlic cloves, finely sliced
1 chilli, finely sliced and
  seeds
1 lemon, zest and juice
170g / ½ cup Basra date
  syrup
Extra virgin olive oil
Maldon sea salt, black
  pepper, and lemon juice
  to serve

Serves 6

Quails are a very generous vehicle for other flavours.
They are not easily overpowered; they love a bit of marinade!
The date syrup in this dish means you get the sweet and the
sour, different things going on that bring it all together. It
adds depth to the flavour. It was speaking to us …

Mix the garlic, chilli, lemon juice and zest, date syrup, olive
oil, and a hefty pinch of salt and black pepper. Set aside.

To spatchcock your quails, use a good pair of kitchen
scissors to simply snip out the back bone (making sure to keep
all fingers clear as you go!). Flatten your quails by pushing the
breast side down onto a board. Add the quails to the marinade
and thoroughly coat in the mix. Leave the birds for at least an
hour, ideally overnight, to soak up the marinade.

Heat up a griddle or, better still, light a barbecue. You do
not want flame – just red-hot charcoal or wood. Preheat the
oven to 180°C / 350°F / gas mark 4.

Once you have the right heat on the griddle or barbecue,
brown the birds well on each side. Pop them into a pan with
the leftover juice and roast in the oven for a further five
minutes to cook through. If the marinade reduces too much,
you can add a little water.

Rest the birds for five minutes and finish with lemon juice.
Serve with juices poured over and plenty of napkins.

Margot Henderson is a
New Zealand caterer, cookery
writer, and co-patron and
chef of Rochelle Canteen and
Rochelle ICA in London.

Puddings and Desserts

Florence Knight

Date pudding and sweet sauce

5g / 1 tsp softened butter
1 tsp loose-leaf Earl Grey tea
4 cardamom pods, crushed
150g / 1 cup bonbon dates
3g / ½ tsp bicarbonate of
  soda (baking soda)
¼ tsp salt
50g / 2¼ tbsp date syrup
70g / ⅓ cup light
  muscovado sugar
40g / ⅓ cup beef suet
1 egg, free range, room
  temperature, beaten
160g / 1½ cups
  self-raising flour
3g / ¾ tsp baking powder

For the sauce
120g / ⅓ cup date syrup
60g / ⅓ cup light
  muscovado sugar
185g / ¾ cup
  unsalted butter
185ml / ¾ cup double
  (heavy) cream
1 tsp sea salt

Serves 6

Bonbon dates are my preferred choice of date for this pudding. The soft sponge hungrily soaks up the sweet sauce.

Preheat the oven to 180 °C / 350 °F / gas mark 4 (or 160 °C / 320 °F fan). Draw around the base of a dariole mould onto greaseproof paper and cut six circles. Butter the moulds and cover each base with the paper. Prepare the same number of foil squares to make lids for the moulds later.

Pour 200ml / ¾ cup boiling water over the tea leaves and cardamom pods. Infuse for five minutes. Destone and roughly chop the dates, place into a bowl with the bicarbonate of soda, and pass the brewed tea through a fine sieve over them. Stir and cover with plastic film to soak for ten minutes.

Combine the syrup, sugar, suet, and egg in a large bowl. Separately, prepare the flour, baking powder, and salt. Blend the dates and liquid to a smooth purée, folding into the bowl of syrup, sugar, suet, and egg. Sieve in the flour mixture, folding until evenly combined. Fill the moulds to two-thirds and cover each with a foil lid. Place them onto a baking sheet, cooking for ten to fifteen minutes until a skewer comes out clean.

While the puddings are baking, prepare the date sauce. Measure the ingredients into a pot. Place over a low heat, stirring every so often to encourage the sugar to dissolve. Once melted, turn up the heat and bring to the boil, reduce the heat, and simmer gently for around ten minutes until the mixture is glossy and thickened. It should coat the back of a spoon evenly. Remove the pan from the heat.

Turn out each pudding and trim as necessary. Place on warm serving plates, ladle over the hot sauce, adding more as they soak it up. Serve with cream or clotted cream.

Florence Knight is a British chef and columnist, best known for her work at the restaurant Polpetto in London.

Cameron Emirali

Sticky date pudding

340g / 2¼ cups
  Medjool dates
2 tbsp bicarbonate of soda
120g / ½ cup butter
160g / ½ cup date syrup
½ tbsp sugar
4 eggs
240g / 2⅛ cups
  self-raising flour
1 tbsp vanilla extract
450g / 2 cups water

For the butterscotch
400g / 2 cups
  muscovado sugar
50g / ¼ cup butter
300ml / 1¼ cups double
  (heavy) cream

Serves 6 (comfortably)

I created this recipe during the first year of my apprenticeship. Over the years, I have tweaked it here and there. This particular version replaces sugar with date syrup, which intensifies the earthiness of the pudding without compromising on sweetness.

Cream the butter, and combine with the sugar and vanilla extract. Add the eggs one by one and then mix in the flour. Meanwhile, boil the dates in water, add in the bicarbonate of soda, and blend with a hand blender. Add this mixture to the cake mix and beat well. Bake at 165 °C / 325 °F / gas mark 3 for twenty to thirty minutes, and then turn the oven down to 150 °C / 300 °F / gas mark 2 to cook for another twenty to thirty minutes.

While the cake is in the oven, you can make a butterscotch by simply combining the sugar, butter, and cream and bringing the mixture to a boil.

To serve, pour the butterscotch into a bowl plate, place the pudding on top, and finish with crème fraîche.

Cameron Emirali is a New
Zealand restaurateur and co-owner
of 10 Greek Street in London.

Yotam Ottolenghi

Pot barley pudding with roasted apples and date syrup

200g / 1 cup pot barley, rinsed
6 tbsp date syrup
3 small cinnamon sticks
Shaved skin of 1 lemon, plus 1 tbsp lemon juice
1½ tsp finely grated nutmeg
¼ tsp salt
3 large Pink Lady apples, peeled, cored, and cut into 2–3cm / 1in pieces
3 medium Bramley apples, peeled, cored, and cut into 2–3cm / 1in pieces
50g / ⅓ cup demerara sugar
50g / ¼ cup unsalted butter, melted
1 vanilla pod, split lengthways and the seeds scraped out
250g / 1 cup plain yoghurt

Serves 4

This is my take on the quintessential British rice pudding. The rice is replaced with pot barley, which gives more texture and lightens this dessert. The caramel-like depth of the syrup goes perfectly with the sweet spices for a Middle Eastern twist.

Pour a litre and a half of water into a medium pan, add the barley, two tablespoons of date syrup, the cinnamon, lemon skin, nutmeg, and a quarter-teaspoon of salt. Bring to a boil, then reduce the heat to medium and simmer for an hour, stirring from time to time, until the barley is the consistency of rice pudding but still retains a bite. Remove and discard the lemon skin and cinnamon, and keep the pot somewhere warm.

After the barley has been cooking for half an hour, heat the oven to 180°C / 350°F / gas mark 4. Mix the apples in a medium bowl with the lemon juice, sugar, butter, vanilla seeds, and pod, then spread out on a large parchment-lined baking tray. Bake in the same oven as the barley for thirty minutes, until the apples are soft and nicely coloured – the Bramleys will be completely soft, while the Pink Ladies should keep their shape. Discard the vanilla pod, gently stir the apples, and set aside somewhere warm.

Divide the warm barley between six bowls and spoon over the apples. Drizzle a teaspoon of date syrup over each portion, top with two tablespoons of yoghurt, and finish with a final teaspoon of date syrup.

Yotam Ottolenghi is an Israeli-British chef, food writer, and owner of the Ottolenghi, NOPI, and ROVI restaurants.

Eleanor Ford

Spiced pumpkin rice pudding

175g / 1½ cups pumpkin
  or butternut squash,
  peeled and grated
80g / ⅓ cup pudding rice
600ml / 2½ cups whole milk
1 tsp ground cinnamon
½ tsp ground cardamom
½ tsp ground cloves
½ tsp ground nutmeg
1 pinch of salt
25g / 1¾ tbsp butter
Date syrup, to serve
Sour cream, to serve

Serves 4

Pumpkin adds earthy sweetness, which complements the caramel-intensity of date syrup. A knob of butter stirred in at the end makes this rice pudding extra creamy. You could brown the butter first if you want a toasted, nutty note.

In a deep pan, combine the grated pumpkin, pudding rice, and milk. Season with the spices and a pinch of salt. Bring to the boil then lower the heat. Simmer uncovered for thirty minutes, stirring from time to time, until the liquid is absorbed and the rice is soft and creamy.

Stir in the butter and sweeten to taste with date syrup. Serve warm with more date syrup drizzled over the top and a dollop of sour cream.

Eleanor Ford is a British food writer
and cookbook author specializing in
Asian and world foods.

Linda Dangoor

Ruz b'haleeb
Date syrup rice pudding

175g / ¾ cup pudding rice
600ml / 2½ cups water
2 tbsp soft brown sugar
Approx. 300ml / 1¼ cups
   whole milk
1 pinch of salt
Date syrup
A few walnuts,
   crushed (optional)
A few raisins (optional)

Serves 4–5

Instead of cinnamon, which is more British, you can make this rice pudding with rose water and make it quite Eastern. Date syrup and walnuts on top are also great.

Wash and drain the rice. Tip it into a large pan, add the water and bring to the boil. Once it starts boiling, reduce the heat to medium and simmer for forty-five minutes or more, until the rice becomes very soft.

Once the rice is very soft, add the milk and a few raisins (if using), simmer on a low heat for another twenty minutes or until the rice mixture is thick. Stir from time to time. If you see that the milk has dried up, add a little more.

Pour into individual bowls, or into one large family bowl. Drizzle abundantly with date syrup and sprinkle some crushed walnuts on top. Serve warm or cold.

Linda Dangoor is an Iraqi artist
and food writer based in London.

Shatha Alimara Najib

Halawat megadi
Beggar's dessert

4 pitta (pita) bread pieces,
  cut into triangles
250g butter
4 tbsp date syrup
¼ cup walnuts to garnish
  (optional)

Serves 4

Halawat megadi is a staple in Iraqi cooking. A simple, economical dessert with a humble beginning – translated as 'beggar's dessert' or 'poor man's dessert' – it was developed as a cheap baklava substitute for the poor at Ramadan. Nowadays beloved by all, this dish can be served alone or with yoghurt or cream; either way, it is always a hit.

Melt the butter in a pan, and fry the pieces of bread at a medium heat to prevent scorching. Once the bread is golden, transfer it onto paper towel to soak up the extra oil. Arrange the bread on a serving plate and drizzle with date syrup to sweeten. Garnish with walnuts and enjoy immediately.

Shatha Alimara Najib is a London-based Iraqi cook and YouTuber.

Shatha Alimara Najib

Knafeh
Shredded filo dough cupcakes

450g / 1lb shredded filo
   (phyllo) dough*
250g / 1 cup mascarpone
300g / 1¼ cups extra thick
   double (heavy) cream
250g / 2 cups
   fresh mozzarella
   (cut into small pieces)
125g / ½ cup butter
½ tsp cardamom
2 tbsp pistachio slices
¼ tsp red food colouring
   (optional)
5 tbsp date syrup

Makes around 16 cupcakes

*The shredded filo is often
   frozen. Leave it to defrost
   for an hour before starting.
   Tearing the shredded filo
   can get messy – best to do
   it over the sink.

The word *knafeh* is derived from the Arabic word *kanaf* (to shelter) and dates back to the tenth century. Today, many households serve *knafeh* to family and friends, from coffee mornings to traditional celebrations. Everyone has their own twist, from raisins to clotted cream and even nutella. My *knafeh* are pink in colour, cupcake sized, and drizzled with date syrup.

Heat the butter in a pan on a low flame until it melts, and then turn off the heat. Add food colouring and cardamom to the pan and leave to cool down.

   Meanwhile, tear, shred, and separate the filo dough strands from each other into a bowl. Once teased apart, add the butter mix slowly to the filo strands; shred again to keep them separated.

   For your *knafeh* filling, mix the mozzarella, mascarpone, and cream together in a bowl.

   Take a small amount of filo (enough to make a ball). Pressing it flat onto your palm, add one tablespoon of filling and cover with a second small amount of filo. You should have something like a cupcake sandwich, with the filling covered.

   Repeat until you have used all the filo and filling, putting each *knafeh* into a cupcake holder. Bake for twenty minutes at 200°C / 400°F / gas mark 6. After seventeen minutes, whip the *knafeh* out to decorate with pistachios before baking for the last three minutes.

   Once out of the oven, drizzle the cakes with date syrup and enjoy hot.

Shatha Alimara Najib is a London-
based Iraqi cook and YouTuber.

Sara Leana Ahmad

Halawat sha'riyyah

4 tbsp butter
350g / 4 cups vermicelli
  noodles, crushed into
  small pieces
230ml / 1 cup hot water
175g / ½ cup date syrup
1 tbsp cardamom
1 pinch of sea salt
40g / ¼ cup pistachios,
  coarsely chopped

Serves 4

This is one of my favourite childhood desserts, on rainy mornings, with my feet up, watching cartoons with my brothers. It is surprisingly simple for something so perfect: sweetened vermicelli noodles. When I was in my early twenties, I discovered that using date syrup with the *sha'riyyah* tasted much smoother than the usual granulated sugar and have never gone back since.

In a deep skillet, melt the butter. Add the vermicelli and mix. Toast the noodles for about five minutes, or until golden. Slowly add the hot water; you may not need to use all of it. Keep stirring, as these noodles get sticky fast. Add date syrup and cardamom, mixing thoroughly. Continue stirring for about five minutes. Remove from the heat and top with pistachios.

Sara Leana Ahmad is an Iraqi-American food blogger at Add a Little Lemon.

Nawal Nasrallah

Easy spicy date sweetmeat

145g / 1¼ cups
  wholewheat flour
340g / 2 cups pitted dates
  (like Medjool or
  Deglet Nour)
125g / ½ cup almond butter
85g / ¼ cup date syrup
1 tsp ground cardamom
½ tsp ground aniseed
½ tsp crushed coriander
  seeds
100g / ¾ cup walnut halves
60g / ½ cup coarsely crushed
  pistachio

Serves 8

This confection was originally pounded with a mortar and pestle (giving it the name *madgouga*, 'pounded'), using a dry variety of dates, called *ashrasi*, along with tahini. The following is my variation on this traditional date dessert. I replace the tahini with almond butter, but feel free to use tahini, peanut butter, or any nut butter of your choice.

Dry toast the flour by putting it in a heavy skillet and stirring constantly until it changes colour and emits a pleasant fragrance (seven to ten minutes on a medium-low heat). Set it aside until it cools.

In a food processor, put the toasted flour along with dates, almond butter, date syrup, cardamom, aniseed, and coriander. Process until mixture forms a ball, about two minutes. If the mixture looks a little dry, add a bit more date syrup.

Divide the date paste into two portions. Generously sprinkle some of the pistachio on a flat surface and press one half of the paste onto it, forming an eighteen-centimetre / seven-inch disc about three-quarters of a centimetre / one third of an inch thick. Make the second disc in the same way.

Put one of the discs on a flat serving plate (pistachio side down), and arrange the walnut halves over the exposed surface. Press the other disc to cover it – pistachio side up this time. Sprinkle generously with pistachio, and gently press all over to help the layers stick together. Neaten up the edges and serve.

Nawal Nasrallah is an Iraqi scholar, food blogger, and cookbook author based in Boston, Massachusetts.

Anissa Helou

Lgeimat fritters

For the fritters
120g / 1 cup plain flour
120g / 1 cup white
  wholewheat flour
1 tsp easy-bake yeast
¼ tsp fine sea salt
1 tbsp sugar
125g / ½ cup yoghurt
1 organic egg

To finish
Vegetable oil for frying
Date syrup to drizzle
  over the fritters

Serves 6–8

Traditionally drizzled with date syrup and probably one of the most ancient Arab sweets, you find these under different names and made slightly differently throughout the Middle East. Some cooks in the Gulf dip them in syrup, which they flavour with cardamom, cinnamon, and saffron instead of the rose and orange blossom water that we use.

To make the batter, mix both flours, yeast, salt, and sugar in a large bowl. Add the yoghurt and 125ml / ½ cup of water. Add the egg and mix until you have a very loose dough or very thick batter. Cover with film and let rest for at least three hours, preferably overnight.

To make the fritters, pour enough vegetable oil into a large pan to deep fry them and place over a medium heat. There are different ways of dropping the batter in the oil, but the easiest is to grab a handful of the dough with a wet hand, squeeze the dough out and use a wet spoon to take off enough of it to drop in the hot oil. When the oil is hot, drop in as many fritters as will fit comfortably. Fry until golden brown all over, stirring all the time to colour them evenly. Remove onto a sieve to let the excess oil drain before transferring to a serving platter. Drizzle as much date syrup as you like without drowning them.

Anissa Helou is a Syrian-
Lebanese chef, broadcaster,
and author of ten cookbooks.

Anna Jones

Instant raw salted caramel chocolate mousse

For the mousse
1 ripe avocado
1 small frozen banana
Juice of ½ lemon or lime
3 tbsp cocoa powder
  (I use the raw stuff)
2 tbsp date syrup

For the salted caramel sauce
8 tbsp date syrup
1 good pinch of sea salt

Serves 2–4

A powerful blender works best here, but failing that, a hand blender and a bit of elbow grease will do just fine. For best results, make sure your banana is frozen and your avocado and lemon are fridge cold. And be sure not to use a really large banana or its flavour will be overpowering.

Get all your ingredients together. Put all the mousse ingredients into a blender with a tablespoon of cold water and blitz on high until everything is whipped to a smooth mousse, stopping to scrape down the sides a couple of times – this may take two or three minutes in a less-powerful blender. Scoop it out into cups and give the blender a quick rinse.

For the caramel sauce, simply mix the date syrup with the sea salt and, if you need, a tablespoon of cold water to loosen. Drizzle the sauce on top of the mousse and top with some extra salt crystals.

Anna Jones is a British cook, stylist, and writer known for her focus on vegetarian food.

Margot Henderson

Yoghurt panna cotta, date syrup, and pomegranate

600ml / 2½ cups buttermilk
400ml / 1⅔ cups double
  (heavy) cream
10 lemon leaves,
  if you can find them
100g / ½ cup sugar
3 bronze gelatine sheets
Date syrup to taste
1 pomegranate, seeds
  and juice

Serves 4–6

Panna cottas are a joyful, simple-to-make family pudding. They also have a sense of fun with their wobbles, but you must make sure you take them out of the fridge for a while before you eat them so they soften a little. The date syrup is an added moreish treat to the whole thing.

Put the cream and lemon leaves into a pan, bring to the boil and set aside to infuse for at least twenty minutes, covered to prevent any evaporation. Strain the cream and put on a low heat. Meanwhile, soak the gelatine in water for a few minutes and add the sugar to the cream. When melted, add the squeezed gelatine and mix until thoroughly combined. Pour through a sieve into the buttermilk and mix gently to combine without incorporating air.

Pour into your desired moulds and put in the fridge to set.

When ready to serve, dip your moulds into some warm water to free the panna cotta from the mould and tip onto your serving plates. Drizzle over a spoonful of date syrup, some pomegranate seeds, and a little of their juice.

Rejoice as it all mixes together as you eat and creates a beautiful mess on your plate.

Margot Henderson is a
New Zealand caterer, cookery
writer, and co-patron and
chef of Rochelle Canteen and
Rochelle ICA in London.

Yvonne Rakowitz

Qemar
Iraqi clotted cream

For the long version
950ml / 4 cups heavy
  whipping cream
950ml / 4 cups buffalo milk
Walnuts or pecans (optional)

You will also need:
3-litre / 3-quart saucepan
Pillowcase
Blanket
Colander

For the short version
500ml / 1 pint heavy
  whipping cream
2 tbsp cornflour (cornstarch)

Serves 4

The way my mother used to make *qemar* took the better part of two days. *Qemar* is a very special dish. It is considered lucky, so it is served on special occasions. When my grandchildren were born, in New York, we had an Iraqi feast, complete with *qemar* and *silan*, our name for date syrup. Here I offer my mother's method and a shorter version.

For the long version, pour the cream and milk into a saucepan and stir. Bring to a slow boil. When you see small bubbles, remove from heat. Place an inverted colander on top of the pan, and then cover with a pillowcase, and then top that with a blanket. Let the pan stand for at least six hours in a warm room, such as a boiler room (which is what we would do). By this point, the cream should have set in a thick skin.

Remove coverings, then – with a knife – gently cut along the perimeter of the saucepan, releasing the skin from the sides of the pan. Carefully remove the skin (that is the treasured *qemar*) with a spatula and refrigerate overnight. Serve with a side of date syrup, bread, and walnuts or pecans (optional).

For the shorter method, pour 250ml / ½ pint heavy cream into small mixing bowl. Add two tablespoons of cornflour (cornstarch) and mix until smooth – make sure there are no lumps! In a small saucepan, heat the remaining heavy cream on a low flame until you see tiny bubbles. Add the cornstarch and cream mixture to the pan and stir well until it thickens.

Pour the mixture into a shallow pan, like a cookie sheet. Cool for two hours and refrigerate overnight. Cut it into pieces, remove with a spatula, and serve with a side of date syrup and bread such as pitta (pita) or baguette. This version serves four; for more or fewer people, adjust accordingly. I always like to make extra and have a little left over for breakfast.

Yvonne Rakowitz, the mother of
Iraqi-American artist Michael
Rakowitz, has worked with her son
to preserve and pass on her family's
Iraqi culture and traditional cooking.

Giorgio Locatelli

Date syrup ice cream, persimmon fruit salad, and chocolate chunky crumble

For the ice cream
535ml / 2¼ cups whole milk
85g / ⅓ cup whipping cream
50g / ½ cup milk powder
40g / 3⅓ tbsp dextrose
20g / 5 tsp caster
  (castor) sugar
120g / ½ cup egg yolk
145g / ½ cup Basra
  date syrup

For the chocolate crumble
220g / 1⅛ cups caster
  (castor) sugar
380g / 1⅔ cups butter
355g / 2⅞ cups plain flour
50g / ⅓ cup cornflour
  (cornstarch)
140g / 1¼ cups cocoa
  powder
1 pinch of table salt

For the fruit salad
2 whole persimmon
60g / 2¾ tbsp
  Basra date syrup
1 vanilla pod

Serves 4

Making ice cream at home is easier than you think. I don't recommend any particular brand of ice-cream maker, but I would urge you to look out for one with a small cylinder and a large motor, because when a motor is very small it gets hot. The quality of the ingredients is also very important – and everything should always be organic. And try to make it in a cool area. If you don't have an ice-cream maker, you can make it in your normal freezer, just stirring it every ten minutes.

Hand blend the milk, cream, milk powder, and dextrose until smooth. Pour the mixture into a pan and cook until it registers 40°C / 100°F. Whisk in the sugar and egg yolk, and add the date syrup. Bring the mixture to 80°C / 175°F, remove it from the heat and cool in the fridge for at least ten to twelve hours. Then stir the ice cream again and pour into an ice-cream maker. Churn to −8°C / 18°F.

For the crumble, mix the butter and sugar in a stand mixer with a paddle attachment, until soft and white. Add the remaining powders, mix into a dough and let it rest for two hours in the fridge. Then roll it between two baking parchments to a thickness of one centimetre / half an inch and bake for fifteen minutes at 170°C / 330°F / gas mark 3. Remove and rest at room temperature, crush into chunks, and store in an airtight container before serving.

For the fruit salad, wash the persimmon, remove the skin and seeds, and cut the flesh into cubes. Place the persimmon, syrup, and the seeds of one vanilla pod in a metal bowl and emulsify everything. Assemble the ice cream, fruit, and crumble, and enjoy.

Giorgio Locatelli is an Italian restaurateur, cookbook author, broadcaster, and chef-patron of Locanda Locatelli in London.

Kitty Travers

Milk chocolate, clotted cream, and date syrup ice cream

500ml / 2⅛ cups whole milk
50g / ¼ cup unrefined sugar
30g / ⅓ cup good-quality
  cocoa powder
15g / 1½ tbsp cornflour
  (cornstarch)
227g / 1 cup clotted cream
  or *qemar* (see page 177)
150g / ½ cup date syrup
1 pinch of sea salt

Makes about 1.2 litres /
  2½ pints or 12 servings

A fudgy chocolate ice cream that was inspired by the traditional Iraqi *qemar*, a kind of clotted cream made from buffalo milk, and date syrup, but that morphed into a kind of meta chocolate milkshake.

In a small bowl, mix two tablespoons of milk with the cornflour (cornstarch). In another large bowl, whisk the clotted cream with the date syrup until smooth.

Whisk the remaining milk with the sugar and cocoa in a medium saucepan. Bring to a boil and simmer over moderate heat, whisking constantly until the sugar dissolves and the cocoa is 'cooked out', about four minutes. Off the heat, gradually whisk in the cornflour mixture. Return to a boil and cook over a moderate heat until slightly thickened, about one minute.

Pour this into the clotted cream, whisking until smooth. Whisk in the salt. Set the bowl in a sink full of ice water, stirring occasionally, for about twenty minutes. Once cool, cover the bowl tightly with film and refrigerate overnight.

Then liquidize the mixture with a stick blender. Pour into an ice-cream maker and churn according to its instructions (around fifteen to twenty minutes, until frozen). Scrape the ice cream into a suitable lidded container. Top with waxed paper to limit air exposure, cover, and freeze until ready to serve.

British confectioner Kitty Travers is the founder of London's La Grotta Ices and teaches at The School of Artisan Food.

Kitty Travers

Coffee bean, almond, and date syrup ice

900g / 3¾ cups water
200g / 1 cup unrefined sugar
1 tbsp date syrup
50g / 1¾oz espresso beans
170g / 1 cup organic white
  almond butter (I use the
  Biona brand)

Makes about 1.5 litres /
  3 pints 3fl oz or 15 servings

A simple method to create a rich-tasting espresso-bean-and-almond slushed ice. The date syrup lends a muscovado sugariness. It is also a vegan dessert, unless you serve it as I like to: smothered with clouds of unsweetened whipped cream. Best eaten the same day or within a few days.

Place a large shallow stainless-steel tray or dish in the freezer to get very cold. In a medium saucepan, heat the water, sugar, and date syrup together, whisking until the sugar dissolves and to a simmer. Immediately remove it from the heat, whisk in the espresso beans and cover the pan tightly with film. Set aside to steep for ten minutes.

Strain the mixture through a sieve into a clean bowl. Discard the beans. Add the almond butter to the warm coffee syrup and blitz with a stick blender. Place the bowl into a sink of iced water to cool, stirring occasionally. Once cold, pour this liquid into the frozen tray and put it carefully in the freezer.

After an hour, the granita should have begun to freeze around the edges. Use a fork to break up any frozen bits and stir them back into the mix, returning every forty-five minutes to repeat. After two to three hours, you should have a slushy muscovado-coloured mix of ice crystals. Serve in chilled glasses with softly whipped cream.

British confectioner Kitty Travers is
the founder of London's La Grotta
Ices and teaches at The School of
Artisan Food.

Tarts, Cakes, and Biscuits

Stephen Harris

Date syrup tart

For the pastry
220g / 1¾ cups plain flour
110g / ½ cup unsalted
  butter, diced and cold
1 egg, lightly beaten
1 pinch of salt

For the filling
450g / 1¼ cups date syrup
1 tbsp chopped stem ginger
75g / 1¼ cups fine
  breadcrumbs
25g / ⅓ cup ground almonds
1 pinch of salt
Grated zest of 1 lemon
Juice of 1 lemon

Thick cream, to serve

Makes one tart (23 cm /
  9 inches across)

I was riffing on a treacle tart with this recipe, but I think the date syrup works better than the traditional treacle. It's a more complex, subtle flavour – and the texture is perfect too.

Put the flour and butter in a food processor and pulse until the texture resembles breadcrumbs. Add the egg and salt, pulsing until the mix has bound together like a dough. Remove the pastry from the blender and finish kneading on a lightly floured surface. Once ready, wrap it in film and chill in the fridge for an hour.

On a floured surface, roll the pastry to a thickness of approximately three or four millimetres / ⅛ inch and line a 23-centimetre / 9-inch tart ring with the pastry. Take a piece of wax paper, scrunch it up, and use it to line the ring over the top of your pastry. Fill the ring with baking beans or rice and bake at 180°C / 350°F / gas mark 4 for twenty minutes. Finally, remove the paper and beans before putting back in the oven to cook to an even, golden brown.

Now for the filling. In a bowl, pour the date syrup and combine with ginger, breadcrumbs, almonds, salt, and lemon. Stir together and pour into the baked pastry case. Bake in the oven at 180°C / 350°F / gas mark 4 for about thirty minutes. Cool slightly and serve with thick cream.

Stephen Harris is a British food writer and chef-patron of The Sportsman restaurant in Whitstable, Kent.

Jeremy Lee

Jefferson Davis tart

For the pastry
340g / 2¾ cups plain flour
1 pinch of salt
120g / ½ cup cold lard
120g / ½ cup cold
  unsalted butter
2 egg yolks
1½ tbsp ice-cold water

For the filling
125g / ½ cup softened butter
100g / ½ cup dark brown
  sugar
2 tbsp date syrup
3 large egg yolks
250ml / 1 cup
  whipping cream
1 tsp cinnamon
½ tsp allspice
⅓ nutmeg, finely grated
14 dates, stoned and
  chopped
60g / ½ cup roughly broken
  pecans or walnuts

This is a favourite recipe from Jane Grigson's *Fruit Book*, which I have always adored. It is slightly modified and a great homage to the humble date.

For the pastry, sift the flour and salt into a bowl. Cut the lard and butter into small pieces and add to the bowl. Swiftly and deftly work the butter, lard, and flour until you get a fine crumb, then add in the egg yolk and ice-cold water and mix into a dough. Knead well, then shape into a round. Wrap and refrigerate for an hour or so. When ready, roll the pastry out to fit a 23-centimetre / 9-inch tart tin, with a slight lip over the edge.

For the tart, mix together the filling ingredients in the order given and gently press into the pastry-lined tart tin. Bake at 200°C / 400°F / gas mark 6 for ten to fifteen minutes, then at 160°C / 320°F / gas mark 3 for a further fifty minutes.

Allow to cool slightly and serve with a generous dollop of double cream.

Jeremy Lee is a British food broadcaster and chef-proprietor at Quo Vadis, London.

Charlie Hibbert

Walnut and date tart

For the pastry
150g / ⅔ cup cold
  butter, cubed
250g / 2½ cups plain flour
75g / ½ cup icing
  (powdered) sugar
2 large eggs, one for
  the pastry and one
  for the egg wash

For the filling
275g / 2⅓ cups walnuts,
  roughly chopped by hand
  into small pieces
200g / ½ cup date syrup
200g / 1 cup dark brown
  sugar
125g / ½ cup butter
3 large eggs, whisked
1 pinch of sea salt
8 large dates, stoned
  and halved (optional)

This will fill a 20cm /
  8in tart case, around
  6cm / 3in deep

Date syrup makes for a perfect sweetener in this recipe. Walnuts work well with dates, their bitterness and crunch contrasting with the soft and sticky fruit. With a spoon of cream and a scoop of ice cream, this is an excellent pudding. Any leftovers will keep for several days in a sealed tin.

Rub the butter into the flour until you have a breadcrumb-like texture. Add the sugar and gently mix before adding one whisked egg. Bring together into a dough, wrap in greaseproof paper, and put in the fridge for at least thirty minutes.

Roll your pastry out onto a lightly floured surface to the thickness of approximately three or four millimetres / ⅛ inch. Line your case, trimming overhanging pastry, and put it back into the fridge to rest for a further thirty minutes.

Preheat your oven to 175 °C / 350 °F / gas mark 4 and whisk the remaining egg. Using a fork, poke a few holes in the bottom of your tart case and line with greaseproof paper before filling with baking beans. Cook for ten to fifteen minutes before removing the beans and returning to the oven for a further five minutes. Remove the paper and beans and wash thoroughly with egg. Flash the tart case through the oven for a minute to cook any eggy residue. Set aside.

Toast the walnuts for five to seven minutes. Meanwhile, warm the syrup and sugar on a low-medium heat until it has come together and the sugar dissolved, stirring occasionally. Allow to cool before stirring in the butter and pouring over the eggs. Add a pinch of salt and the walnuts, and mix gently. Fill the case as close to the top as possible and decorate with halved dates. Cook for thirty to forty minutes and allow to settle before serving with whipped cream and (coffee) ice cream.

Charlie Hibbert trained under Jeremy Lee at Quo Vadis in London and is Head Chef at the Ox Barn at Thyme, in Gloucestershire.

Rosie Sykes

Oat and apple slice

150g / 1⅞ cups rolled oats
  (I favour the less-processed
  jumbo ones)
150g / 1½ cups plain flour
150g / ⅔ cup butter, melted
75g / ⅓ cup golden
  caster (castor) sugar
75g / 3½ tbsp date syrup,
  plus extra for adding to
  the fruit
50g / ⅓ cup almonds,
  roughly chopped
50g / ½ cup pistachios,
  roughly chopped
500g / 1lb 2oz apple, a
  mixture of cooking and
  eating, cored and peeled
  (though I leave the peel on
  if it is a thinnish red skin)

This is delicious served warm and can be made with other types of fruit depending on the time of year. The oats are a delicious foil to the date syrup. You can also switch the variety of nut you use depending on the fruit.

Preheat the oven to 180°C / 350°F / gas mark 4. Line a loose-based tart case (around 20 centimetres / 8 inches across) with buttered baking parchment. Mix together the oats, flour, and sugar, before adding in the date syrup and melted butter. Mix to a sticky dough, and use two-thirds of the mixture to make a base in the tart tin. Press it down very well and scatter the apples over, along with a couple of tablespoons of date syrup.

Add the nuts to the remaining third of dough still in the bowl and mix together well. Scatter over the top of the apples in an even layer before placing the oat and apple slice in the oven to cook until light golden brown (approximately thirty to thirty-five minutes).

Eat straight away with cream or custard, or leave the slice to cool to enjoy alongside a cup of tea or coffee.

Rosie Sykes is a British chef and food writer.

Alice Waters

Date galette Chez Panisse

For the galette dough
250g / 2 cups
  unbleached plain flour
¾ tsp caster (castor) sugar
10 tbsp unsalted butter,
  chilled, coarsely chopped,
  slightly softened
¼ tsp salt

For the filling
300g / 2 cups pitted Barhi or
  another variety of soft dates
1 tbsp unsalted butter, melted
60g / ½ cup walnuts,
  coarsely chopped
Zest of ½ orange
125ml / ½ cup freshly
  squeezed orange juice
1 tsp orange blossom water
1 tbsp date syrup
3 tbsp butter, melted,
  for brushing
50g / ¼ cup caster (castor)
  sugar

Dates have some kind of symbolic and magical aspect to them. We made this galette in the earlier days of Chez Panisse. It is exciting to discover it again, and to use date syrup.

Combine the flour and sugar with the salt in a bowl. Add butter, toss to coat, then flatten with thumb and forefinger. Drizzle over a 60ml / ¼ cup of chilled water, and incorporate the water until the dough starts to come together.

If there is unincorporated flour, drizzle chilled water over, one tablespoon at a time, raking until it looks moist and ropy with very little dry flour. Divide into two balls, wrap in film, press lightly into discs, and refrigerate for at least one hour.

Process the dates in a food processor for one minute, or chop finely to a coarse paste. If the dates remain too chunky, add a little milk to soften the paste. Transfer the purée to a medium bowl, add butter, walnuts, zest, juice, orange blossom water, date syrup, and a pinch of salt, and mix well.

Roll out the discs of dough on a lightly floured surface to 36-centimetre / 12-inch rounds, around 5 millimetres / 2 inches thick. Brush off any excess flour, then transfer to a large tray lined with baking paper and refrigerate for thirty minutes.

Preheat oven to 200 °C / 400 °F / gas mark 6. Spread the date mixture over one disc, leaving a 2.5-centimetre / 1-inch border. Brush the border with water, then cover the galette with the other round. Press edges together, trim an edge all the way around, then crimp with a fork or pinch with your fingers. Cut a few decorative slits for steam to escape during baking. Brush the top of the galette generously with melted butter, sprinkle sugar evenly over, and bake on a pizza stone on the floor of the oven or the lowest rack until browned, thirty to forty minutes. Cool to room temperature before serving.

Alice Waters is an American restaurateur, activist, author, and executive chef and founder of Chez Panisse in California.

Thomasina Miers

Sticky date, tahini, and cardamom cake with toffee-date sauce

100g / ⅔ pitted Anjoman
  or other good-quality dates
250g / ¾ cup date syrup
  plus 80g / ¼ cup extra for
  the icing
120g / ⅔ cup tahini
180g / ¾ cup unsalted
  butter at room temperature,
  plus 20g / ¾oz extra
  for greasing the tray
120g / ⅝ cup soft brown
  sugar
4 eggs
100g / ⅝ cup walnuts,
  roughly chopped
200g / 1¾ cups
  self-raising flour
2 tsp baking powder
½ tsp ground cardamom
  seeds
¼ tsp freshly grated nutmeg
½ tsp salt

For the sticky toffee sauce
60g / ¼ cup butter
150g / ⅜ cup date syrup
200g / ⅞ cup double
  (heavy) cream

This gently spiced, moist cake is sticky, unctuous, and decidedly naughty. I like it with large dollops of crème fraîche to add a creamy silkiness.

Heat the oven to 160°C / 320°F / gas mark 2½. Grease a 24-centimetre / 9-inch square baking tray (or equivalent) and line with parchment.

Put the dates, date syrup, and tahini in a bowl and blitz to a purée with a stick blender, adding two tablespoons of water to help loosen the mixture. Meanwhile, cream the butter and 180g / ⅜ cup of sugar together using a wooden spoon, or an electric beater, until light and fluffy. Beat in the date mixture, followed by the eggs, one at a time. Finally, stir in the walnuts.

Weigh out the flour, baking powder, spices, and salt together into a bowl. Sift into the wet mixture, stirring in between sifting, until all the ingredients are fully incorporated. Pour into the baking tray and bake for fifty-five to sixty minutes, until a knife comes out almost, but not completely, clean.

While the cake is baking, make the sticky sauce. Put the butter and date syrup into a small saucepan and stir over a medium heat until completely combined. Stir in the cream. Serve slices of the sticky, light sponge with the warm sticky toffee-date sauce.

Thomasina Miers is an English cook, writer, television presenter, and co-founder of the Wahaca restaurant group.

Brett Redman

Olive oil, yoghurt, and date syrup cake

250g / 1 cup yoghurt
125g / ½ cup extra
  virgin olive oil
  (choose a fruity one)
150g / ⅜ cup date syrup
Zest of 1 lemon
3 large eggs
190g / 1½ cups plain flour
1 tsp baking powder

A moist, slightly gooey-textured cake. It is nothing like traditional sponge, but the fruity olive oil combined with the savouriness of the date syrup makes for something otherworldly. This is equally as good as a dessert at a serious dinner party or eaten as part of a quick afternoon tea.

Heat the oven to 180 °C / 350 °F / gas mark 4. Using oil, lightly grease a 23-centimetre / 9-inch round cake or springform pan and line the bottom with parchment paper. If you are using a cake pan, then grease the paper too.

In a large bowl, whisk together the yoghurt, olive oil, date syrup, and lemon zest. Add the eggs, one at a time, and whisk until the mix is light and fluffy. Sift in the flour and baking powder. Use a rubber spatula to fold through until most of the lumps are gone, being careful not to overmix.

Pour the batter into the pan and spread it out evenly. Bake for roughly forty-five minutes, or until the top is lightly browned and a skewer comes out clean.

Place the cake on a cooking rack for ten minutes. Once cool, remove it from the pan by running a knife around the edge. Lastly, take a plate and flip the cake onto it and then back onto the rack.

Slice and serve with the date syrup and extra yoghurt.

Brett Redman is an Australian restaurateur and chef of Jidori and Elliot's in London.

Sarit Packer and Itamar Srulovich

Ginger and date cake

150ml / ⅔ cup double (heavy) cream

150g / ⅜ cup date syrup (or black treacle), plus more to glaze (if you like)

50g / ¼ cup unsalted butter

100g / ½ cup soft dark brown sugar

200g / 1¾ cups self-raising flour

2 tsp ground ginger

2 tsp ground cinnamon

½ tsp ground cardamom

½ tsp table salt

130g / ⅞ cup pitted dates, chopped

50g / ¼ cup crystallized ginger, chopped, plus more to garnish (if you like)

1 egg

Makes a 1kg / 2lb cake

This cake embodies the best of traditional British baking: it is dark and moist, glistens with syrup, and is perfumed with all the spice of a Dickensian Christmas. But at the same time, the flavours are Middle Eastern: ginger, cinnamon, cardamom, and sweet dates. This perhaps is the happy meeting point for our country of origin and our adopted one.

Preheat the oven to 180°C / 350°F / gas mark 4 (160°C / 320°F fan). Butter a 1-kilogram / 2-pound tin and line with baking parchment to cover the base and sides, allowing a little overhang.

Warm the cream, date syrup, butter, and sugar together in a large saucepan until the sugar has dissolved and the mixture is just starting to boil. Remove from the heat and stir in the flour, spices, and salt. Mix in the chopped dates and ginger, add the egg, and combine before transferring the batter to the tin.

Bake for thirty minutes, then turn the tin around and leave for another thirty minutes. If you push down a little with the tip of your finger in the centre and it does not sink, remove from the oven. Otherwise, you can bake for a further ten minutes – but no more! As soon as it is out, brush with the extra date syrup (if using) and leave to cool.

To finish, decorate with more crystallized ginger tossed in caster (castor) sugar. This cake is even better the day after baking, and lasts well in an airtight container.

Chefs Sarit Packer and Itamar Srulovich run London's Honey & Co., Honey & Smoke, and Honey & Spice.

Vicky Graham

Sticky toffee baked donuts

220g / 1½ cups dates
1 tsp bicarbonate of soda
350ml / 1 cup hot water
90g / ⅜ cup unsalted butter
155g / ⅞ cup caster (castor) sugar
1 tbsp date syrup
2 eggs
170g / 1½ cups self-raising flour
1 tsp mixed spice
1 tsp ground cinnamon
¼ tsp salt
2 tbsp Ovaltine powder
2 tbsp natural yoghurt

For the salted caramel glaze
125g / ½ cup unsalted butter
150g / ¾ cup golden caster (castor) sugar
50g / ¼ cup dark muscovado sugar
50g / 2¼ tbsp date syrup
150ml / ⅔ cup whole milk
350g / 2⅔ cups icing (powdered) sugar
½ tsp salt

Makes 12–14 donuts

Sticky toffee is arguably the best British pudding of all time, and these baked donuts offer a slightly lighter, less dense version of the original, complete with a super silky caramel glaze that makes it impossible to have just one.

Preheat the oven to 180°C / 350°F / gas mark 4 (160°C / 320°F fan), grease ring donut tins, and set to one side. Place the dates in a bowl, add the bicarbonate of soda, and pour the hot water over. Leave to soak for a couple of minutes before draining, and then whizz in a food processor or roughly chop with a knife. Beat the sugar and butter together until fluffy, add the date syrup, and mix again.

Combine the flour, mixed spice, cinnamon, salt, and Ovaltine in a bowl. Add an egg and a spoonful of the dry mixture into the wet ingredients and beat until combined. Repeat for the second egg, gradually adding the rest of the dry ingredients to the bowl spoon by spoon, and then fold in the chopped dates and yoghurt. Place a tablespoon of the mixture into each of the greased donut rings, level out with a clean spoon until each is two-thirds full, and then bake for eleven to fourteen minutes.

While they are baking, make the salted caramel glaze by placing the butter and sugars into a pan and on a medium heat until the butter has melted and the sugar has dissolved. Add the milk and salt and stir again. Mix three-quarters of the caramel mixture into the icing sugar slowly, stirring all the time. Once it becomes a thick paste with no lumps, gradually add the remaining caramel mixture and keep stirring.

Remove the donuts from the oven. Once cool, tip from their tins and dip in the salted caramel glaze to finish.

Vicky Graham is a British cookbook author, chef, and creative force behind London bakery Vicky's Donuts.

Caroline Eden

Green Farm parkin

110g / ½ cup unsalted
 butter, softened
100g / ½ cup soft
 dark brown sugar
25g / 3½ tsp black
 strap molasses
110g / ⅓ cup golden syrup
80g / ¼ cup date syrup
200g / 2¼ cups medium
 stone-ground oatmeal
120g / 1 cup self-raising flour
40g / 1½oz crystallized
 ginger, chopped into
 pea-sized pieces
2 tsp ground ginger
1 tsp mixed spice
1 generous pinch of salt
2 large eggs
1 tbsp milk

I spent a couple of years living in a remote sheep-farming community in North Yorkshire called Green Farm. It was cold, draughty, and damp, but the views, hill walks, and welcoming pubs were magical. It was then that I discovered Yorkshire parkin, a hearty, sticky cake ideal for taking on hikes. Here, date syrup adds an extra layer of sweetness.

Preheat the oven to 150°C / 300°F / gas mark 2. Grease a 20 by 20-centimetre / 8 by 8-inch square tin with butter, line the bottom with parchment, and then grease that too.

Gently heat the butter, sugar, and all the syrups in a saucepan, being careful not to boil. Once melted and mixed well, remove from the heat and set aside. Next, in a large bowl combine all the dry ingredients, including the salt. Add the melted syrups and thoroughly mix with the dry ingredients. Finally, add in the eggs and milk, mixing well until all are combined and you have a thick batter.

Pour into a greased tin and bake for an hour. When the parkin is ready, it will come away from the sides slightly, be springy on top, and a skewer should come out clean.

The key with parkin is patience: store in its baking tin – or a cake tin – wrapped in greaseproof paper or foil for a minimum of two days before cutting it. This allows its deep flavour and stickiness to develop fully. When it is ready, I like to cut mine into sixteen mini squares.

Caroline Eden is a British food
and travel writer focusing on the
countries of the former Soviet
Union and south Asia.

Niki Segnit

Double-life date parkin
with hot date and cream sauce

For the parkin
200g / 1⅔ cups plain flour
1 tsp bicarbonate of soda
100g / 1¼ cups oatmeal
1½ tbsp ground ginger
2 tsp mixed spice
A few pinches of salt
100g / ½ cup butter
100g / ½ cup soft
  brown sugar
200g / ½ cup date syrup
1 egg
100ml / ⅜ cup milk

To make one 20cm / 8in
  square cake

For sauce (optional)
50g / ¼ cup butter
200ml / ⅞ cup double
  (heavy) cream
4 tbsp date syrup
A few pinches of salt

This is adapted from a popular Yorkshire recipe. You are supposed to keep the cake wrapped for a week before you cut it, allowing it to reach proper northern levels of moistness. Alternatively, wrap half of it, cutting the other half into squares while still warm and serving with a hot date and cream sauce. Like sticky toffee pudding, only fruitier. And as with sticky toffee pudding, a scoop of vanilla ice cream or crème fraîche can only improve matters.

Heat the oven to 160°C / 320°F / gas mark 3.

In a bowl, measure out the plain flour, bicarbonate of soda, oatmeal, ground ginger, mixed spice, and a few pinches of salt. Mix and make a well in the centre.

Measure the butter, soft brown sugar, and date syrup into a saucepan and place over a medium heat, stirring intermittently until the sugar and butter have melted. Pour into the dry ingredients and stir until thoroughly combined. Beat the egg with the milk and mix into the batter. Pour into a greased, 20cm / 8-inch square cake tin and bake in the centre of the oven for thirty-five to forty minutes. Once cooled, wrap the cake, and try to wait five days before cutting it.

If you are serving the cake pudding-style with the sauce, put the butter, cream, date syrup, and salt into a pan and bring to the boil over a medium heat. Simmer for a few minutes, stirring, then pour into a jug to serve on the warm squares of cake. This will make enough sauce for four to five portions.

You can also add chopped dates to the batter. You might reduce the ginger and add freshly grated nutmeg or ground cardamom. The grated zest of two large oranges will give a pleasingly bitter riposte to the cake's sweetness. The cooled cake can be given a thin glacé icing. Vanilla, rose, or orange blossom water are excellent pairings for the date and ginger.

Niki Segnit is a British food writer and author of The Flavour Thesaurus.

Niki Segnit

Date syrup and walnut snaps

50g / ¼ cup butter
50g / 2¼ tbsp date syrup
50g / ¼ cup light
brown sugar
50g / ⅜ cup plain flour
50g / ⅜ chopped walnuts

Makes 8–10
palm-size biscuits

These are very thin, crisp, praline-like biscuits, not unlike ginger snaps or florentines, but darker and more toffee-flavoured thanks to the substitution of date syrup for lighter, blander golden syrup. Cream-cheese ice cream is the perfect accompaniment, but I also make mini versions to serve with coffee or a strong drink after supper. They take all of about fifteen minutes to make, and are easy to commit to memory, calling as they do for equal weights of the five ingredients.

Heat the oven to 180°C / 350°F / gas mark 4.

Measure the flour and chopped walnuts into a bowl. Add a pinch of salt and mix. Measure the butter, date syrup, and sugar into a saucepan and warm through, stirring intermittently. Remove once the sugar has dissolved.

Pour the hot, buttery syrup into the flour and mix. While the mixture is still warm, use two spoons to transfer small dollops – about two teaspoons each – onto a prepared baking tray, then flatten and neaten them. Allow room for the mixture to spread as it bakes. Bake for eight to ten minutes, remove the tray, and let the biscuits harden for about a minute before using a palette knife to transfer them to a cooling rack. They will stay good and snappy for a few days if kept wrapped in an airtight box.

Use white or dark brown sugar in place of light brown. The former will lend less flavour, but will keep the biscuits snappier for a little longer. You might prefer to use chopped pistachios, pecans, almonds, or a mix, to leave the nuts out altogether, to add even more, or to use a mix of nuts and dried or glacé fruit. Or you could spice them up. Ginger, cinnamon, mixed spice, and cardamom are all classic partners for dates. I might add a few pinches of fennel seeds to play against the sweetness. A vegan variation can be made by substituting an appropriate solid vegan fat for the butter.

Niki Segnit is a British food writer and author of *The Flavour Thesaurus*.

Olia Hercules

Date syrup and curd biscuits

80g / ⅓ cup butter
200g / ⅞ cup cottage cheese
  or Polish *twaróg*
50g / 2¼ tbsp date syrup
200g / 1⅔ cups plain flour
1 tsp baking powder
50g / ¼ cup demerara sugar

Makes 20 biscuits

In my part of Ukraine – the south, where watermelons are king – people used to make watermelon molasses. Sugar was scarce after the war, so huge vats of watermelon juice were reduced in massive cauldrons into something we called *bekmez*. Women used to make this 'watermelon honey' for sweet baking, and I like to use date molasses – that is, date syrup – in a similar way.

Mix the butter, cheese, and date syrup together. Sift the flour and baking powder together and then stir into the cheese mixture. Knead the dough briefly and then chill it for at least thirty minutes.

Preheat the oven to 180°C / 350°F / gas mark 4 and line a large baking tray with silicone paper. Flour a surface well before rolling the dough out into a sheet to a thickness of approximately three or four millimetres / ⅛ inches. Stamp out 8-centimetre / 3¼-inch circles with a glass or a cookie cutter – you can keep rerolling the offcuts to make more.

Sprinkle demerara sugar over the biscuits and press gently to make sure it sticks. Then fold the circle in half and press one of the sides into the sugar again. Then fold again and press into the sugar for the last time. Bake on your large tray with silicone paper (leaving some distance in between, as the biscuits will expand slightly) for about twenty minutes or until golden on top.

Olia Hercules is a London-based Ukrainian chef, food writer, and food stylist.

Philip Juma

Kleicha
Date and cardamom cookies

600g / 1lb 5oz
   plain 'OO' flour
200g / 1 cup
   melted margarine
7g / 2¼ tsp dry
   yeast (1 sachet)
1 tbsp sugar
½ tbsp salt
200–300ml / ⅞–1¼
   cups water
2 tbsp nigella seeds
150g / ⅜ cup Basra
   date syrup
3 tbsp sunflower oil
1 tbsp cardamom
2 large sandwich bags
   (cut open)
1 egg

For the date paste
500g / 3¼ cups dates
   (stone out)
300ml / 1¼ cups
   boiling water
1 tbsp cardamom
1 pinch of bicarbonate
   of soda

or 600g / 1lb 5oz
   packet of date paste

Makes 40 biscuits

Philip Juma is an English-Irish-Iraqi
food writer and founder and head
chef of JUMA Kitchen in London.

Traditionally served in our house over Easter and Christmas, this date cookie is a massive favourite of mine. I could eat mountains of them with a chai or coffee. Kleicha is made with a walnut filling or a date filling – both are equally delicious. You can buy a pre-packed date paste, but making your own is always best.

In a food mixer, add the flour, melted margarine, yeast, and sugar. Add the salt, ensuring it is far away from the yeast, as they cancel each other out.

On a low setting, mix the ingredients together aiming for a pizza-dough texture. Add water gradually. When you feel it is close, add the nigella seeds. There should be a spring in the dough, and it should feel moist when ready. Place in a bowl and cover with a towel; leave to rest for forty minutes.

In a large pan, pour the boiling water over the dates. Add a pinch of bicarbonate of soda and leave on a low heat for thirty minutes. Add the cardamom and stir occasionally. Once the dates have broken down, place in a food processor until you get a smooth consistency. Add more water if needed and scrape down the sides to ensure all of it is blended.

Now separate your risen ball of pastry into four. Roll each piece into a rectangle on a floured surface. Position the longest side vertical and the shortest horizontal to you. Spread your date mixture on top of the pastry.

Begin from the vertical side and roll tightly from right to left. Take your rolled pastry and cut the kleicha as you see fit – traditionally, they are 5 to 7 centimetres / 2 to 3 inches. Brush with beaten egg and bake in the oven for twenty minutes (until golden) at 180°C / 350°F / gas mark 4. Repeat for the other three batches.

Preserves, Condiments, and Cocktails

Asma Khan

Spiced cranberry chutney

8cm / 3in cinnamon stick
4 whole green cardamoms
1 tsp whole cloves
2 hot green fresh chillies
8cm / 3in orange peel
350ml / 1½ cups water
300g / ⅞ cup date syrup
100g / ⅔ cup pitted dates
500g / 5 cups fresh
  (or frozen) cranberries

Makes around 3 jars

This cranberry chutney is similar to one made with an Indian berry, *ber* (sometimes called Indian plum or *jujube*), which is traditionally cooked with generous quantities of *khajur gur* – date palm jaggery. Many early traders from the Middle East and Persia made their bases in Calcutta, and there is clearly a link between the Bengal jaggery and the region's Arab influence.

Boil the cloves, cinnamon, cardamom, green chillies, and orange peel in water. Once the water comes to a boil, lower the heat and simmer for twenty minutes. Strain the water, remove all the spices, and put the infused water back on the heat. Add the dates and date syrup and bring the water back to a boil. Then lower the heat and simmer for another fifteen minutes. Add the fresh cranberries and cook for a further ten minutes till the berries pop. Serve at room temperature.

Asma Khan is an Indian writer, entrepreneur, and founder of Darjeeling Express in London.

Claudia Roden

Thirteenth-century preserve of dates stuffed with almonds

Iraqi dried dates
Almonds or pistachios
Date syrup
Honey
Saffron
Musk
Rose water

Quantities are not specified in original recipe.

Preserves of dates stuffed with almonds, pistachios, or walnuts are made in different parts of the Arab world. I was thrilled to find this description of the same preserve, but made with dried dates, in a thirteenth-century recipe from Baghdad featured by Charles Perry in his book *Medieval Arab Cookery*.

✿

'Wash Iraqi dried dates in hot water and remove the pits and replace them with almonds or pistachios. Boil syrup and honey and skim. Then throw the dates in, and when it has come to the boil twice, leave it until it is cold. Colour with saffron and flavour with musk and rose water. It will have a good consistency, and it is nice.'

Claudia Roden is an Egyptian-British cookbook writer and cultural anthropologist.

Marcus Samuelsson

Date and raisin chutney with date syrup

4 tbsp vegetable oil, divided
6 pitted dates, chopped
6 dried apricots, chopped
2 garlic cloves, minced
2.5cm / 1in piece of ginger,
  peeled and minced
½ poblano chilli, seeded
  and diced
2 tbsp pine nuts
2 tbsp sesame seeds
1 orange, zest and juice
1 tbsp brown sugar
2 tbsp date syrup
2 tbsp raisins
120ml / ½ cup red wine
60ml / ¼ cup
  balsamic vinegar
1 tbsp adobe paste
4 slices bacon, diced
1 tsp garam masala
1 tsp turmeric
1 tbsp chopped fresh
  coriander (cilantro)

You know, it is amazing to work with something like a date that has such an ancient history, and I really thought about that when I came up with this recipe. This chutney incorporates date syrup as well as dates themselves. You can use it as a garnish on a meat dish or just eat it with flatbread as a snack.

Heat two tablespoons of oil in a medium saucepan. Sauté the pine nuts and sesame seeds until golden brown. Season with salt, garam masala, and turmeric. Remove from the saucepan and reserve in a bowl to the side. In the same pan, add the bacon and cook until it is fully cooked.

Add the garlic, poblano, and ginger and sauté until soft – about seven minutes. Add all the remaining ingredients except the coriander (cilantro). Simmer on a low heat until the liquid has been absorbed. Season with salt, remove from heat, and then fold in the coriander.

Marcus Samuelsson is an Ethiopian-Swedish restaurateur, and head and executive chef, respectively, of Red Rooster and Aquavit restaurants in New York.

Nasrin Rooghani

Garlic *torshi*

4 heads of garlic (around 400g / 14 oz), cloves separated and peeled
500ml / 2⅛ cups vinegar (approximate, to cover the ingredients) – red wine vinegar adds colour; date vinegar if possible
1–1½ tbsp date syrup (or to taste)
2 tsp whole green cardamom pods
1½ tsp nigella seeds
1½ tsp (whole) black peppercorns
1½ tsp (whole) pink peppercorns (optional)
1½ tsp salt (or to taste)

The ingredients for the pickling liquid can be scaled up or down; just make sure that you have enough vinegar to cover the cooking garlic.

Torshi is the name given in Iran to any pickle. Here, the garlic cloves are simmered gently in order to soften them, then sweetened with date syrup for extra nuance of flavour and depth of colour. Leave in a cool place for a few hours, days, or even a whole week before serving.

Put all the ingredients together in a pan so that the vinegar easily covers the garlic. Bring to the boil and then turn down the heat and leave to simmer, very gently, until the garlic is just becoming tender – not soft or in danger of falling apart. This may take anything from half an hour to a couple of hours, depending on the garlic and how gentle the simmer; test regularly with the tip of a small, sharp knife. When it is ready, turn off the heat, transfer to a sterilized jar, and leave to cool.

To store the *torshi* for any length of time, keep refrigerated (although it is best served at room temperature). Garlic *torshi* will serve as an accompaniment to almost any meal. Serve with the lamb Baharat on pages 116–17 and rice, or wrapped in bread. Shred the lamb, lay over some flatbread, scatter sliced or whole garlic *torshi* on top, together with some sliced radish (for crunch), drizzle with tahini sauce, and sprinkle with a generous covering of herbs – coriander, dill, mint.

Nasrin Rooghani is an Iranian chef with the social enterprise Mazi Mas in London.

Soli Zardosht

Persianesque garlic pickle
with date syrup

170g / 1 cup garlic
cloves, peeled
150ml / ⅔ cup
red wine vinegar
100ml / ¼ cup balsamic
vinegar
¼ tsp coriander seeds, dry
toasted in a small pan
1 tsp salt
2 tbsp date syrup

Makes one 370g / 13oz jar

Seldom is a Persian *sofreh*, or spread, laid without at least
two types of pickles. For us, a well-balanced *torshi* not only
brings acidity, but also rounds off each mouthful with an added
layer of flavour that completes a meal. This recipe is my take
on the traditional method where whole heads of garlic are
fermented in vinegar until soft. The combination of date syrup
with the other vinegars makes for a sweet and tart pickle that
will be great served alongside fish, stews, and in wraps.

Begin by washing and sterilizing the jar and lid – you
can do this by placing both in a preheated oven set at
140°C / 275°F / gas mark 1 for ten minutes. In the meantime,
put all the ingredients except the date syrup in a small non-
reactive saucepan and bring to a boil. Turn down the heat
immediately and leave the mixture to simmer gently for fifteen
minutes. Turn off the heat and use a slotted spoon to transfer
all the garlic to the sterilized jar. Pour the infused vinegar
over the garlic and into the jar, leaving approximately 1.5 to
2 centimetres / ⅝–⅞ inch empty space from the top. Add the
date syrup, screw the jar shut tightly, and give it a gentle shake
to mix. Store in a dark and cool place for two weeks, after
which time the pickle is ready to eat.

Any leftover infused vinegar can be stored for future pickling
or used in salad dressings.

Soli Zardosht is an Iranian-British
chef, running Zardosht with sister
Sanaz across residencies in London
and New York.

Brett Redman

Airmail cocktail

3⅞ tbsp Cuban rum
2 tbsp lime juice
1 tbsp date syrup
35ml /1⅛fl oz champagne

Originally, I thought date syrup would work only with dark spirits and in an Old Fashioned-style drink, but it surprised us all by adding a complex savoury note to an Airmail, our signature champagne cocktail.

Shake the rum, date syrup, and lime juice with ice in a cocktail shaker. Strain through a fine strainer into a flute and top up with the champagne. Drink fast!

Brett Redman is an Australian restaurateur and chef of Jidori and Elliot's in London.

Russell Norman

Medjool date Old Fashioned

75ml / 2½fl oz excellent
  bourbon
1 tsp date syrup
Angostura bitters
Large slice of orange peel,
  pith removed
1 Medjool date

Makes 1 cocktail

The Old Fashioned is one of my favourite cocktails. This version with a Middle Eastern twist is a great alternative and a real winter warmer. It's perfect as a digestif after a celebratory meal.

Fill a cocktail shaker with ice and pour in the bourbon, then add the date syrup and two shakes of angostura bitters.

Using a long-handled bar spoon, stir vigorously twenty times clockwise. Strain into a whisky tumbler filled with fresh ice. Rub the orange peel around the rim and drop into the drink. Garnish with the date.

Russell Norman is a British
restaurateur and food writer.

Silan Ruminations   Ella Shohat

Our eager rush to the jar filled with the smooth-flowing syrupy liquid sweetened many a childhood at a time when chocolate still had the flavour of a foreign luxury. Our cravings were satisfied on the spot by the blend of date honey and sesame paste, called *'dibis wa rashi'* and in our Jewish-Baghdadi-Arabic *haqi* (dialect) *'silan wu-rashi'*. Preparing the savoury mixture was also an exercise in visual pleasure, as the pouring of the brownish liquid over the beige substance in the *shekkasa* (bowl) fascinated us with its fast-forming spiral. The neighbouring Levantine culinary transformation of the sesame into the now world-famous sour tahini, meanwhile, felt alien to our palate, which viscerally associated the paste with the familiar honeyed syrup.

But for me, the interflow of the *silan* and the *rashi* came to a post-dessert climax when my father would carry me on his back as if I were a *jud* (hot-water bottle), while he rhythmically recited the refrain: *''ala dhahri jud el-mai, 'ala dhahri jud el-mai...'* ('On my back is the hot-water bottle'). As the steps of *abuyi* (my dad) accelerated into jumps, so did the pace of the refrain. And I would have to hug his neck even tighter, sometimes pulling, whether accidentally or not, on his quivering double chin as our commingled laughter filled the air. The ritual would inevitably end with the filial *jud* reluctantly and awkwardly sliding down to the sofa or onto the Persian rug.

In a house full of relatives and friends, *abuyi* would play the *kamanja* (violin), alongside his frequent guest Salim, nicknamed *al-'uwad* (the oud player) to distinguish him from the many other Salims in our lives. And together they would form a *chalghi*, an ensemble playing *maqam* music. And as the *hafla* gathering would sometimes last into the wee hours, the adults, anticipating the morning nourishment, would express their melancholic affection for Iraq's breakfast staple of *qemar*, a cream made out of *jamus* (water buffalo) milk served with *mraba* (jam) or *silan*. In our exile in the biblical land of milk and honey, *qemar* was not readily available, and invariably someone would give expression to this frustrated craving, proclaiming in what might have sounded like a curse: '*Inhajam betu el-hatha el-qemar el-akelnanu b'Beghdad*' ('May the house of that *qemar* we used to eat in Baghdad be destroyed.'). But, in fact, the phrase was a form of praise, albeit in an upside-down manner, of the intensity of their desire, as if nothing could ever compare to their quotidian sunrise delight.

This oxymoronic homage gave voice to their yearning for the homes they had been forced to abandon and to their lives in the land of 'the waters of Babylon'. But in retrospect, how could they have even begun to imagine that the world from which they had departed would come to face a very literal destruction some four or five decades later? How could they then have pictured Iraq's pollution of air, water, and earth from depleted uranium, poisonous chemicals, and toxic smoke that would end up wreaking havoc on their millennial place of belonging? The 'shock and awe' bombing of industrial plants has by now spoiled ground water and damaged sewage-treatment sites, contaminating rivers, drinking water, and local vegetation dating back to Mesopotamian antiquity. And yet in all the present-day exilic places to which so many Iraqis, of diverse backgrounds, have been dispersed, we are also aware of those who have remained and have continued to cultivate their orchards, even amid ongoing ruination, even in the face of the catastrophic liquidation of ecological equilibrium, cultural inheritance sites, and human lives.

For us, far away from Iraq, the *dibs al-tamer / silan* cans that preserve the syrup made out of the indigenous date palms (*nakhlat al-tamer*), and which now journey all the way to London, Sydney, and New York, offer a small consolation: a piece of *bilad al-rafidayn* (the land between two rivers) in our many elsewheres across the seas.

A can of date syrup, a gift to the author from Michael Rakowitz, now placed on a pot of palm fronds grown from the pits of Medjool dates. Photo: Ella Shohat, New York, October 2016.

Ella Habiba Shohat is an author from a Jewish-Baghdadi family. She is professor of cultural studies at New York University.

Afterword   Justine Simons

As Michael Rakowitz writes in his introduction, this book
seeks to extend the space of the artwork that he produced
in 2018 for the Fourth Plinth in London's Trafalgar Square.
A sculpture made from food cans is a first for the plinth.
But, as with most great art, it is not as simple as it sounds.
Scratch below the surface and we realize that the sculpture is
a powerful statement about the impact of war. As we know,
this beautiful monument made from date syrup cans is a
recreation of the Lamassu, a winged bull that had stood at
the entrance of Nineveh (now Mosul) in Iraq for almost three
thousand years from 700 BC until it was destroyed by ISIS
in 2015. But valuable historical monuments are not the only
things destroyed by war; they also decimate local economies.
In Iraq, the industry for date syrup, a Middle Eastern staple,
also collapsed as a result of the various wars in recent
decades. However, the popularity of Michael's sculpture
The invisible enemy should not exist with the public continues to
demonstrate the power that art has to connect, communicate,
and transform.

The sculptures on the Fourth Plinth always relate to
their environment. So what is it that connects London's
pre-eminent public square with this sweet, dark molasses?
Well, Trafalgar Square is a place where the nation comes
together to celebrate, to commemorate, to protest, and to
mourn. War is part of its story too. The square itself is a
monument to a British victory in the Napoleonic Wars, and
there are military leaders on its other plinths. More recently,
it was one of the focal points for the anti-war movement
of February 2003, when in a series of coordinated protests
around the world up to eleven million people in more than
sixty countries marched in opposition to the then imminent
Iraq War.

Today, the square is a place to celebrate the city's
extraordinary diversity; through cultural events, national
holidays, and often food, showing that, as the slogan goes,

'London is Open' to all. This Fourth Plinth commission has also travelled beyond the boundaries of Trafalgar Square. During Autumn 2018, Michael cooked date syrup recipes in community kitchens and schools across London to connect more Londoners with his project.

Food, like art, is universal. It has the power to connect people across geography, language, and culture, something that Michael has always recognized and made integral to his work. Like a beautiful meal, significant art places us all around the same 'table': it nourishes us, stirs our memories, and brings us together.

pages 234–5
Michael Rakowitz's sculpture
The invisible enemy should not exist,
which will stand upon the Fourth
Plinth for two years until March 2020.

Justine Simons OBE is Deputy
Mayor of London for Culture and
the Creative Industries.

Michael Rakowitz and the publishers would like to thank the following individuals, groups, and organizations for their assistance and support in creating this book.

Mayor of London
Northwestern University, Evanston, Illinois
Galerie Barbara Wien, Berlin
Jane Lombard Gallery, New York
All of the contributors who generously provided recipes
Claudia Roden
Ella Shohat
Justine Simons OBE
Linda Dangoor
Philip Juma
Sam and Sam Clark and all the team at Moro
Margot Henderson
Refettorio Felix, Kensington
Gayhurst Community School, Hackney
Elizabeth Garrett Anderson School, Islington
Mayor of London's Culture team: Jo, Kirsten, and George
Olia Hercules and Joe Woodhouse
Caroline Irby
Grimshaw family
Rakowitz family

MAYOR OF LONDON | **FOURTH PLINTH.**

All photographs are by Joe Woodhouse, except:
pp. 6, 10–11, 18 (top), 20–3, 80–1, 112–13, 148–9: Caroline Irby
pp. 13–17, 238–9: courtesy Michael Rakowitz
p. 233: courtesy Ella Shohat
pp. 234–5: courtesy Greater London Authority

The photograph on pp. 238–9 is from Michael Rakowitz's *Every weapon is a tool if you hold it right: An Enemy Kitchen Masgouf Cookout*, 2014. It features fish caught and prepared by Iraqi refugees and US veterans, bayonets used by Iraqi and US soldiers, and the Chicago flag in Iraqi colours, an unofficial symbol made for the Iraqi expatriate community of the city.

The recipes on pp. 41, 61, and 173 are reproduced by permission of HarperCollins Publishers Ltd. Copyright © 2019 Anna Jones.

The recipes on pp. 79 and 111 are reprinted from *Morito* by Samantha Clark and Samuel Clark, published by Ebury Press. Reproduced by permission of The Random House Group Ltd. Copyright © 2014.

The recipe on p. 159 is adapted from one in *Samarkand: Recipes and Stories From Central Asia and the Caucasus* by Caroline Eden and Eleanor Ford, published by Kyle Books.

The recipes on pp. 207 and 209 are copyright © Niki Segnit and reproduced by permission of the author c/o Rogers, Coleridge & White Ltd., 20 Powis Mews, London W11 1JN.

First published in the United Kingdom in 2019 by Art Books Publishing Ltd in association with Plinth

Art Books Publishing Ltd
18 Shacklewell Lane
London E8 2EZ
Tel: +44 (0)20 8533 5835
info@artbookspublishing.co.uk
www.artbookspublishing.co.uk

ISBN 978-1-908970-49-7

Creative director: Chloe Grimshaw
Editor: Emily Watkins
Food styling: Olia Hercules
Food photography: Joe Woodhouse
Drawings: Michael Rakowitz
Design: Patrick Fry

The endpapers have been produced from bespoke date-syrup-and-tahini marbled paper created by Jemma Lewis Marbling and Design

Printed and bound in Latvia by Livonia

Distributed outside North America by
Thames & Hudson
181a High Holborn
London WC1V 7QX
United Kingdom
Tel: +44 (0)20 7845 5000
sales@thameshudson.co.uk

Available in North America through
ARTBOOK | D.A.P.
75 Broad Street, Suite 630
New York, N.Y. 10004
www.artbook.com

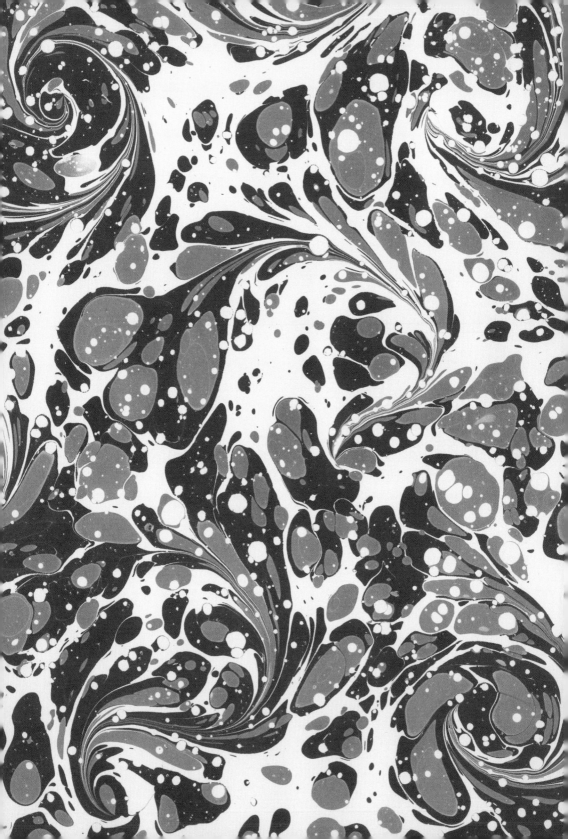